BOGS,
MEADOWS,
MARSHES,
& SWAMPS

BOGS, MEADOWS, MARSHES, & SWAMPS

A Guide to 25 Wetland Sites of Washington State

by Marie Churney and Susan Williams

THE
MOUNTAINEERS

Published by
The Mountaineers
1001 SW Klickitat Way
Seattle, Washington 98134

0 9 8 7 6
5 4 3 2 1

Published simultaneously in Canada by Douglas & McIntyre, Ltd., 1615 Venables Street, Vancouver, B.C. V5L 2H1

Published simultaneously in Great Britain by Cordee, 3a DeMontfort Street, Leicester, England, LE1 7HD

Manufactured in the United States of America

Edited by Ellen O. Setteducati
Illustrations by Jim Hays
Maps by Virtual Design
All photographs by the authors
Cover design by Helen Cherullo
Book design by Alice Merrill
Cover photograph: Bullfrog in lily pond © Stacey Green, Tony Stone Images

Frontispiece: Scriber Lake City Park

Library of Congress Cataloging-in-Publication Data

Churney, Marie.
    Bogs, meadows, marshes, and swamps : a guide to 25 wetland sites
 of Washington State / by Marie Churney and Susan Williams.
        p.   cm.
 Includes bibliographical references (p.   ) and index.
 ISBN 0-89886-476-3
 1. Wetland ecology—Washington (State)—Guidebooks.   2. Wetlands—
 Washington (State)—Guidebooks   3. Washington (State)—Guidebooks.
 I. Williams, Susan, 1954 Aug. 24–   II. Title.
 QH105.W2C49   1996   96-1206
 574.5'26325'09797—dc20   CIP

♻ Printed on recycled paper

TABLE OF CONTENTS

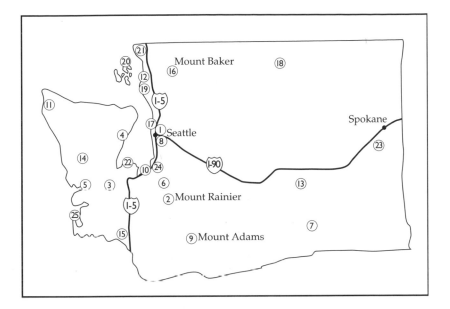

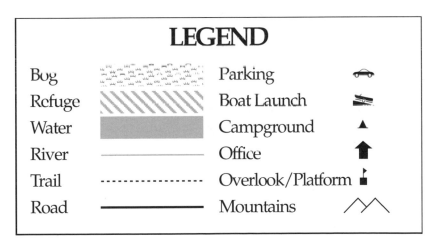

LEGEND

Bog		Parking	
Refuge		Boat Launch	
Water		Campground	▲
River		Office	
Trail		Overlook/Platform	
Road		Mountains	

PREFACE

Nearly a million acres of freshwater, estuarine, and marine wetlands can be found in Washington. The Department of Ecology lists wetlands ranging in size from a few to 9,000 acres. Wetlands constitute less than 3 percent of the 44 million acres of land mass in the state as a whole, but their impact is felt well beyond their geographic extent. It is our hope that the information we have compiled, through field observations; extensive reading of the scientific literature on wetlands; and conversations with biologists, naturalists, land planners, wetland specialists, realtors, and environmentalists, will enhance your awareness and enjoyment of these fascinating, endangered, and critically important biological communities.

The authors are indebted to John Norton, who provided the material on fish, and to the many individuals who provided information and advice about wetland issues. We appreciate the helpful comments from Dr. Terry Ford, Dr. John Main, and Dr. Richard McGinnis, and the indefatigable support of The Mountaineers Books staff.

This book is dedicated to Katherine and Mat Mottola, exemplary stewards of the land, whose ethic of living harmonizes with the tenor of the natural world.

INTRODUCTION

The state of Washington has over two hundred wetland areas that are accessible to the public, but because information about wetlands is not readily available outside scholarly journals or textbooks, few people really understand or appreciate them. Many good references and guides exist for walkers, boaters, and cyclists, but none concentrates specifically on wetlands. This book is intended to fill that gap.

HOW TO USE THIS BOOK

Take this book with you as you tramp about getting your feet wet and inadvertently providing a meal for developing young mosquitoes. Use it to help interpret the wetland landscape—an intriguing mixture of land and water—and to help you identify the plants and animals commonly found in Washington's wetlands. There are many kinds of wetlands in this state, and all are worth exploring.

Some of the wetland sites discussed fit the classic definition of a wetland, while others may stretch your sense of what constitutes a wetland. In any case, visiting many types of wetlands will expand your sense of the different communities of plants and animals and the conditions under which they live, and it has the potential to hone your sense of the joy in experiencing a unique dimension of the natural world. Wetlands are an endangered community—they deserve greater attention and appreciation. We hope that this book will heighten that appreciation.

This book is divided into three sections. The first part describes major wetland communities, and the second provides descriptions of twenty-five trips to observe these communities. Each trip includes a map and a site description, directions to the site, pertinent information on seasonal changes, and a description of the natural features that may be seen. Many wetland walks have no distinct trails and are best approached with a wander-and-look attitude. All of the walks described have public access; a few are meant to be boat trips or are best approached from the water, but most are designed as self-guided walking tours. The third section contains descriptions of plants and animals commonly encountered in these wetlands.

WHAT TO TAKE

Above all, be prepared to get wet—remember where you are! If it isn't raining, it probably has been or will be, and underbrush and emergent plants are often dripping wet. Wear rubber boots or old tennis shoes to protect your feet. Hiking boots are seldom necessary.

You might want to include a jacket, a hat, first-aid supplies, a flashlight, a good sunscreen, and lunch in your day pack. Insect repellent is useful. Long sleeves help keep the mosquitoes away, and binoculars allow you to enjoy areas you are unable to approach. A spare plastic bag and tie give you something in which to carry out any litter that you find. You might want to carry a compass; it could preclude your circling the same clump of cattails more often than you might choose. A hand lens or magnifying glass reveals a scale of structure and beauty invisible to the naked eye, and wetlands are an excellent place for a camera. Wetlands are good places to sketch your observations; a waterproof pad and pencil might come in handy.

It takes time to see things happening, and while the plants are readily visible, many visits may be necessary before the resident animals are observed. There are field guides available for almost every category of organism and inanimate feature: insects, plants, animals, animal tracks, trees, rocks, mosses and lichens, and pond life. There are also guides for specific areas such as the Cascades and the Olympics. The National Audubon Society has published a wetland guide, and some of the society's other books, such as those on grasslands and marine life, may also have application here. Refer to the Further Reading section for a list of other useful publications.

MAPS

The overall map gives the general location of all the wetland walks listed in this book. Please refer to the individual descriptions for specific directions on how to reach each site. The maps for each walk were compiled from on-site information and USGS maps; they outline the general terrain and highlight the important natural features. Some of the wetlands do not have structured trail systems, but at the least a general map or a photo is provided for each site.

Wood duck house at Skagit Delta

SAFETY

Use common sense and caution: wetlands can be deceptive. Bogs often appear firm but may give way underfoot, pond edges drop off quickly, and rocks and logs or other obstacles are hidden underwater or behind dense plant growth. Mud flats may at first seem firm but can hide soft holes where even adults can get stuck—all water-saturated ground can quickly become soft and dangerous. Boardwalks and bridges are slippery more often than not. Children should be supervised at all times; they are often deceived by the depth of the water and can quickly slip down muddy slopes.

Animals sometimes appear tame, and one's inclination is to reach out to them; restrain yourself. Even when fed by humans, wild animals are wild. They very reasonably resent your violating their space and may be quick to bite or slash. Keep a good distance between your children and the inhabitants of wetlands, and the ground will be laid for a future day of observations.

There are many familiar berries growing in wetlands, and while they may be safe enough to eat, this is not the place for experimentation. There are also some potentially dangerous plants you might encounter here. Water-hemlock is not uncommon in marshes, but because the roots are the most poisonous part of the plant, it is an unlikely candidate for human poisoning. Poison hemlock, however, is always a risk with children, since its aerial parts look like wild carrot or parsley. Although not a problem to touch, this plant is potentially lethal if the seeds are chewed and swallowed; in such a case, immediate medical attention should be sought.

ETIQUETTE

When you enter a wetland, you are entering someone else's home, and it is important not to change that home and make it unlivable. Make your passing unmarked and the damage will be minimal. Some wetlands, such as bogs, are extremely fragile, whereas wet meadows can tolerate much more traffic. Stay on maintained trails or boardwalks; don't forge your own trail, since this is an invitation for others to follow.

Leave flowers, plants, and animals there for others to enjoy. Many wetland plants are protected, and even a small amount of collecting can quickly eliminate a plant from the immediate area. Photographs are a good substitution for collections, and they have the added advantage of providing an environmental context for the organism. As in any other outdoor area, carry out your litter, and through your own respect for our natural areas, be an example to your children and friends.

A NOTE ABOUT SAFETY

Safety is an important concern in all outdoor activities. No guidebook can alert you to every hazard or anticipate the limitations of every reader. Therefore, the descriptions of roads, trails, routes, and natural features in this book are not representations that a particular place or excursion will be safe for your party. When you follow any of the routes described in this book, you assume responsibility for your own safety. Under normal conditions, such excursions require the usual attention to traffic, road and trail conditions, weather, terrain, the capabilities of your party, and other factors. Keeping informed on current conditions and exercising common sense are the keys to a safe, enjoyable outing.

The Mountaineers

PART 1
THE WETLANDS OF WASHINGTON

Salt Marsh

THE WETLANDS OF WASHINGTON

On the edge of a marsh on Lake Kapowsin, a motionless blue heron patiently waits for minnows to explore the stems of its feet. Rising fog obscures the landscape and bird calls echo over the water as gnats swarm up and down in the warming air. The sharp odor of decaying vegetation drifts by. Cattails dip and weave as red-winged blackbirds choose nesting sites and squabble over bird concerns. A garter snake slips into the water, while brilliant blue dragonflies hover over lily pads. Mosquito larvae snap to the surface to take in air, then drift safely to the bottom. Swallows snatch the hatching mosquitoes as they become airborne. Around the edges of the marsh, water-filtering clumps of bulrushes, with their distinctive sharp points, give way to shrubs, and an occasional tree marks the slow invasion of forest from the high shore—evidence of the gradual change of this aquatic world to squishy, semidry land. Creatures living beneath the surface of the water enjoy stable water temperatures, and as the plants flourish and decline, their decay releases nutrients for the survival of other organisms. Food abounds here, and life is good.

The abundant wetlands of both eastern and western Washington are home to countless similar scenes. At the Nisqually Delta salt and fresh water mingle and create warm nurseries for young fish, while the insects welling up from the marsh provide food for hundreds of birds. Along the Kent Valley, heron families grow up in the midst of construction sites and road-building projects. Lower a kayak into the water and drift down the Duwamish River and you will see the plant and animal species change with the transition from fresh water to salt. Barnacles in this brackish water mark the strong influence of the daily tidal wash on Seattle's industrial waterfront. In eastern Washington ducks and geese settle to feed in sky-washed marshes, while the shallow ponds that spread across thousands of acres in this often arid land provide a resting place for clouds of other migratory species.

All wetlands share the function of holding and absorbing water as it moves through the environment in a continuous cycle: evaporating into the atmosphere, riding the wind up and over the mountains, and then raining down the slopes to gather in fast-moving mountain streams and rivers. Full of glacial milk (rock so finely ground by glacial pressure that it stays suspended in the water and turns it gray-white) and soil scoured from the landscape, this rapidly moving water slows as it

Kapowsin Floating Bog

encounters a wetland—its force absorbed as if by a giant sponge. But the actions of humans increasingly intervene in this natural cycle. A bulldozer appears, huge trucks drop mountains of fill, and another wetland is paved over to make room for a shopping mall. We dredge out sediment for a marina or ignore a flood plain and build another subdivision. These activities rearrange the landscape and then seal it over, preventing it from performing the functions to which it has adapted over the millennia. Among the results are increased flooding and periodic high volumes of runoff. Fortunately, we have begun to recognize that we need to find a better way to interact with these irreplaceable natural landscapes.

WHAT IS A WETLAND?

Wetlands form wherever the water table is either at or near the surface of the land: on the inside bends and former channels of a river, in the shallow braidings of a creek spreading out on a river delta, or where streams trickle slowly through flat land. Wetlands are amphibious worlds, places where land and water mingle, creating an invigorating challenge to their many plant and animal inhabitants. They are transitional areas where the land is either covered by shallow water or periodically inundated when seasonal rains saturate the soil. Here the primary plant life consists of hydrophytes—plants that have a high tolerance for living with their roots submerged in water or water-saturated soil. Swamps, marshes, bogs, estuaries, and wet meadows are all wetlands, but each of these specific types of wetland is defined by the communities of plants and animals typically associated with it. The presence of a particular plant or set of plants, the so-called indicator species, is one clue in determining both the presence and the identity of the wetland. Skunk cabbage is an indicator species: its presence tells the observer that the ground is moist—it has standing or seeping water most of the year; if it didn't, that plant couldn't live there.

Another identifying characteristic of wetlands is the presence of hydric soils. An important parameter in classifying a soil as hydric is a week of continuous surface soil saturation. This produces anaerobic (low-oxygen) conditions in the soil and influences the growth and survival of the plants on that site. Soils with low oxygen contain toxic forms of manganese, iron, and sulfur, which also affect plant growth. Soils that remain waterlogged for at least a month during the growing season develop two distinctive features: gleying and mottling. These features reflect wetness in mineral soils. A gleyed soil is blue, gray, or green and is created by minerals, particularly iron and manganese, in solution. Formed in the absence of air in water-saturated mineral soils, this gleyed soil may be interspersed with mottles. Mottles are evidence of oxidation along root channels and in other parts of the soil. They are yellow-to-reddish-brown blotches. If it is not clear how long a particular piece of land has been inundated, taking a soil sample and looking for gleying and mottling settles the issue concerning the presence of hydric soil.

Lack of oxygen is also characteristic of wetlands. Water holds little oxygen compared to soil, which has extensive pore space between its particles. When soil is flooded with water, this oxygen reserve disappears. Furthermore oxygen dissolves and diffuses into water or saturated soil very slowly. As a result many plants cannot survive in the wetland environment. Those plants that do live in wetlands have solved the problem of low oxygen availability in various ways. Plants living in water have particularly well-developed areas of spongy tissue—enlarged intercellular cavities that form a continuous system of gas passageways by which the roots can exchange oxygen with the air. Other water plants may have only a thin leaf covering, rather than a heavy cuticle, which allows oxygen and other gases to move more freely between the plant and the water. Leaves below water may adapt in other ways; they may be divided into very fine leaflets, and thus have more surface area available for oxygen exchange.

FUNCTIONS OF WETLANDS

Wetlands perform many important functions. They help to replenish groundwater by slowing the movement of water downhill, giving it time to percolate through the soil. The millions of tiny mud and silt particles suspended in their waters act as a sieve that helps remove pollutants, including chemicals and excess nutrients released by water treatment plants. They can absorb huge quantities of water, contributing to flood control by helping to moderate the difference between high and low water levels. Wetland vegetation stabilizes shorelines, reduces erosion, and contributes to land formation. The warm, shallow water at the edges of wetlands provides a nursery for young fish and a source of food and shelter for other wildlife.

Wetlands stabilize shorelines. Plant stems provide a buffer against the erosive power of storms hitting coastal marshes. The first 8 feet of a marsh absorb half of a storm's wave energy (the force with which a wave pounds the shore), and by the time these waves have traveled 30 feet into the marsh, nearly all of their energy has been absorbed. As the waves lose their power, they drop their load of soil, and the marsh grows seaward, sometimes at the rate of 1½ inches a year. This suggests that the effects of storms and flooding could be greatly reduced if marshland growth were enhanced through the planting of marsh grasses, in lieu of expensive public protection schemes involving bulkheads, ditching, and dredging. As deltas and valleys become cultivated, we often forget that these plains are the buffers between mountains and oceans, between upland forest drainage systems and the marine coast. They have absorbed both water and sediment for thousands of years in a cycle of flooding and soil deposition. Houses, commercial structures, and parking lots that we insist on placing here are sometimes inundated with soil-laden water when the naturally absorptive capacity of the wetland is modified and sealed off with pavement.

Both marine and freshwater wetlands accumulate sediment, clearing the water and improving water quality. The more slowly the water moves, the greater the sediment load dropped. This process of sedimentation is clearly illustrated by any river delta. As the water flows through

Typical plant species found in the moist understory of a forested swamp

vegetation, even more sediment is trapped, reducing the necessity for downstream dredging of channels and bays. When dredged materials are put back onto the marshland, smaller particles are removed before the water returns to the main channel. Clearer water, greater light penetration, and the subsequent growth of phytoplankton—tiny suspended plant life—result. The complex food webs of the marshes and channels thrive, and fish and waterfowl multiply.

Pollutants are filtered out of water passing through wetlands. Wetlands remove some of the nitrogen and phosphorus that run off agricultural land. Without some kind of filtration, this nutrient-rich water encourages population explosions of algae and other plants. This massive plant growth and subsequent decay contribute to oxygen deprivation in lakes and ponds and often threaten or kill residents such as invertebrates and fish. The plants absorb the phosphorus for cell growth;

both nitrogen and phosphorus are also absorbed by the bacteria living on the substrate surface.

Along with nutrients from this water, marsh grasses absorb heavy metals, pesticides, and other toxic compounds. Although these substances are taken up into plant tissues, it is probable that they are modified before becoming part of the residue of plant stem decomposition. This happens as the toxins are broken down into other compounds or absorb other materials into their structure.

Wetlands provide wildlife with a source of food and shelter. Some mammals visit to drink water and gather food, while others, such as beaver, muskrat, and mice, live there. Birds rest in safety and feed in the warm shallows. Wetland vegetation provides birds with nesting opportunities. Migratory birds count on tideland rest stops such as Willapa Bay and Dungeness Spit to restore necessary energy during long north and south flights. Anadromous fish—migratory ocean species that spawn in fresh water—reproduce in freshwater streams and mature in shallow bays. Estuaries are best seen as vast nurseries where invertebrate populations explode, providing food for young fish and birds.

Decomposers play an important role in the movement of energy throughout the wetland community. Being large creatures ourselves, we tend to think of large animals as the most significant part of any food chain. Their size is misleading in determining their importance in energy flow in the ecosystem because their numbers are few, whereas the organisms that are largely responsible for the decomposition of dead plants are found in vast numbers, cover a huge surface area, and have a significance well beyond their size. Detritus feeders—also known as shredders—transform dead plants and animals into smaller and smaller particles and release them to be reincorporated into other organisms.

WETLAND COMMUNITIES

There are many systems for categorizing living communities, and wetlands are known by many names depending on where you are geographically and on whether you are describing the landscape or writing regulations. Swamps, for example, can be dominated by trees or by shrubs, and either would be called a swamp in the United States. In the plains states a marsh is called a wet prairie. In Europe the same wetland would be described as a fen, a kind of peat-accumulating marsh that is non-acidic. Bog, fen, peatland, mire, moor, and muskeg are all terms that have been applied to bogs. Salt marshes can be separated into high pickleweed marsh, short cordgrass marsh, and the intertidal zone, with normal high tides and low tides. The divisions depend on the purpose of the classification system.

The communities included here were chosen because they are the most significant in terms of their impact on the landscape. Other communities that could have been added to this list include inland alkaline ponds, vernal pools, and riverine communities. Inland saline or alkaline systems are found primarily on arid interior land. High temperatures, poor drainage, and weathering rocks and soils, which release soluble salts into the water, create salt flats. These salt flats are populated by halophytes, plants that flourish in salty soil. Animal inhabitants often include the microscopic brine shrimp, able to survive in salt and endure the total absence of water. Vernal pools are found in both coastal and inland areas. They occur when rain accumulates in shallow depressions and creates a short-lived oasis—usually a springtime event. Even this small collection of water encourages the growth of quick-blooming, fast-seeding annuals and perennials. Atkins Lake, in Douglas County, is such a phenomenon; with heavy rains, it may cover nearly 100 acres. Rivers are important landscape features; as living communities, however, they tend to grade into some of the selected community types such as forested swamps, freshwater marshes, and salt marshes.

All of the six communities described here—bogs, eelgrass beds, forested swamps, freshwater marshes, salt marshes, and wet meadows—are readily observed in Washington State. In the field, they do not always exhibit tidy characteristics, inevitably merging with each other and with the rest of the landscape. Natural systems are not static, and as more water or more silt is added to a wetland system, the frequency of specific plants and animals may shift, giving it a new appearance.

BOG

An early summer morning on a bog is a delightful experience. The pungent odor of peat fills the air as the observer floats gently on a mat of moss, surrounded by silence and a landscape of unusual plants.

Pacific Northwest bogs exhibit classic traits. Usually situated on the edge of a shallow pond, a bog is characterized by poor drainage and minimal inflow of water. Bogs are made up of several zones. Along the edge of open water a floating mat of rushes and sedges is surrounded by mounds of sphagnum (peat moss) and cranberry plants. This in turn is surrounded by a shrub zone containing swamp laurel and Labrador tea, which grades into a forest of hemlock, sometimes interspersed with birch. Many bogs are also surrounded by a marginal ditch that never fills in and is lined with wetland shrubs, such as hardhack and willow.

The most characteristic bog plants are the peat mosses. They are the most primitive of the mosses and also the most common, covering about 1 percent of the earth's land mass. Canada alone is more than 18 percent peatland. Peat mosses are of special interest ecologically because they modify their environment. Peat moss tends to grow in cold and slow-moving water, where it soon exhausts the oxygen and nutrients and in the process acidifies the water (most bogs have an acidic level of 4; an orange is about 3.5). Few other plant species can tolerate these conditions, so the peat moss becomes dominant. In addition, very few of the bacteria that cause plant decomposition can survive in such an environment; therefore, dead peat moss accumulates rather than being decomposed. Peat buildup can suffocate plants, and many bog plants have specialized roots that allow them to rise above the problem by elevating their shoot bases as the peat accumulates.

Lemming

Like wetland plants in general, bog plants demonstrate many solutions to waterlogging, including a reduced need for oxygen, the development of special between-cell spaces for oxygen storage, and the leakage of oxygen from roots to produce a locally aerobic environment. Many bog plants move nutrients from leaves to roots before their leaves fall, thereby conserving the nutrients for reuse. Some bog plants have very deep roots with which to transfer nutrients to the surface.

The slow decomposition typical of bogs also means that the next generation of bog plants has fewer nutrients available to it. Lacking contact with mineral surfaces or an influx of less stagnant water, bogs acquire most of their nutrients from rainfall, with phosphorus and potassium often less available than nitrogen.

Ericads, members of the heath or rhododendron family, are the most common bog shrubs. Throughout the Pacific Northwest, Labrador tea abounds. In Alaska, British Columbia, and Washington, but not in Oregon, swamp laurel is common. Another ericad, small cranberry, is a dominant species in sphagnum bogs. Pacific gentian and cotton grass characterize bogs and seldom grow outside them.

Another plant found in Washington bogs is the sundew, a carnivorous plant that traps insects on the tips of its glistening hairs. Insectivory—the ability of carnivorous plants to trap and digest insects—demonstrates a fascinating supplement to chlorophyll-produced food. Although insectivorous plants trap and digest insects, they are not dependent on them for nutrients and will be perfectly healthy without them.

Animals that live in bogs are few in both number of species and number of individuals. The physical character of the bog and the sometimes extreme seasonal and daily oscillations in temperature require special adaptations. This means that a species that can live in a bog often cannot live anywhere else.

The dominant plant eaters in bogs are mainly insects. Insect species uncommon elsewhere in the Pacific Northwest may be very common in bogs. One example is a ground beetle thought to be rare in Washington but very common in a bog near Seattle. A primitive yellow-and-black dragonfly is unique to the Pacific Northwest. It lives mainly in bogs on the Olympic Peninsula but is also found in Cascade mountain bogs. Instead of the more usual aquatic larvae, it has terrestrial larvae that burrow into the peat layer of the bog.

Larger omnivores and herbivores that frequent bogs include grouse, rodents, and occasional large mammals such as deer, elk, and bear. Predators such as owls, weasels, frogs, and birds tend to live on the fringes of the bog.

Peat bogs are useful to archaeologists. The very slow rate of decomposition has preserved ancient wood and artifacts of every kind, even human bodies. A burial pool in Florida has yielded more than 160 bodies estimated to be around 7,000 years old. In this case, skin and hair were not preserved, but textiles, wooden objects, brain tissues, and stomach contents were. Well-preserved human remains have frequently been found in European bogs. Perhaps the most famous is the 2,000-year-old Tollund Man, who was found in Denmark in 1950 and whose well-preserved body features and clothing provided much information about his lifestyle.

EELGRASS BED

Sensuous leaves lap and slither around your legs as you walk through a partially submerged eelgrass bed. Feeling your way along the muddy substrate, you hope the resident Dungeness crab senses your approach and moves away instead of holding her ground. Other creatures also live here—shrimp snap against your legs as they hurry to shelter; buried in the mud, soft-shell clams endlessly filter the water for food, revealing themselves with small volcanoes of mud. Snails wander up and down the eelgrass blades as they scrape off whole forests of algae for dinner.

Eelgrass beds grow on mud flats, which consist of an underlayment of grains of sand and minute particles of organic matter—fine material formed by the wear of tides on the landscape and by deposits of soil pulled from the surrounding highlands. Burrowing animals use the plentiful organic matter in this mud. Vegetation on mud flats consists of large plants such as eelgrass and surfgrass, but the tiniest organisms create the greatest biomass—dense, slimy mats of diatoms. Miniature sculpted boxes of silica enclose these microscopic organisms. While diatoms form a significant part of the food chain in this habitat, transported detritus—bits of dead plants and animals washed in from other sources—is the greatest source of energy.

Eelgrass at low tide

The major seed-producing plant on tide flats is eelgrass. Eelgrass grows in sheltered water on gravel, in firm sand, or in soft mud, in slow currents. (Padilla Bay, Willapa Bay, and Grays Harbor in Washington and Netarts Bay in Oregon display the largest eelgrass beds in the Pacific Northwest.) Normally it does not grow below 22 feet (because of inadequate light penetration) or where the salinity drops below twenty parts per thousand. It extends up into river mouths only as far as the reach of the daily tides.

From horizontal rhizomes buried in the mud, eelgrass sends vertical shoots up into the water. Each of these shoots measures up to 8 feet long and bears from four to six leaves each year as well as submerged flowers that are fertilized by pollen drifting through the water. The leaves and shoots form an underwater forest that by baffling the water currents and increasing the deposit of sediment provides a sheltered habitat for a variety of organisms.

Eelgrass leaves provide the basis for a complex food web. They are home to brown algae, protists, diatoms, and bacteria, which often makes them feel as if they're covered with felt. In addition, shrimp, jellyfish, squid, and fish rest on the leaves; ducks and shorebirds use them as a food source; and Pacific herring, smelt, and snails deposit their eggs (which are in turn eaten by fish fry) on the blades. This entire parade starts with an alga, and until it begins to grow neither bacteria nor diatoms will attach themselves. Although the mobile members of this community can move on to other feeding grounds, the lifespan of the attached organisms is completely dependent on the eelgrass. Furthermore, as the eelgrass changes form with the seasons, it affects the amount of detritus that is deposited as well as the density of the underwater forest's leaf cover; both of these in turn influence the animal community.

Unfortunately, the larger, more conspicuous members of this community are also commercially attractive. Two shrimp, the broken-back and the coonstripe, live here, along with Dungeness crab, English sole, and starry flounder. Although crab numbers are low, their size ensures a recognition of their presence in the community—as any Dungeness crab

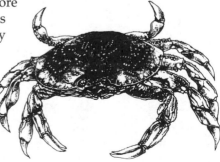

Dungeness crab

hunter knows, an eelgrass bed is the best place to look. Red rock crab move in and out of the area as well. Eelgrass beds contain large populations of soft-shell clams and crab, which live in association with worms, snails, shrimp, and other invertebrates. The favorite food of juvenile chum salmon, a microscopic invertebrate, also lives here.

Found in this habitat are shrimp, blennies, bogies, sea catfish and filefish, sea-run cutthroat trout, five species of salmon, steelhead, smelt, Pacific herring, sole, flounder, and ten species of sculpins. Numerous stages of sea bass, rockfish, sea bream, greenling, squid, and crab occur seasonally in this community. Puffers are transients. Most of these organisms are carnivores that move in and out of the beds to feed on organisms recycling detritus. Eelgrass beds are particularly important for the juvenile stages of many organisms in that they provide food and shelter during their development. Regardless of the species noted, the numbers of fish species associated with eelgrass are significantly higher than those found in adjacent unvegetated mud flats. A total of forty-one species were found in an eelgrass bed at Alki Point, while sixty-four species of fish were reported from northern Puget Sound.

Eelgrass beds are heavily used by birds; they may eat the vegetation itself or feed on seeds and crustaceans, mollusks, and worms. Heavy deposits of herring eggs on the grass attract gulls and surf scoters. When the tide is out, shore birds such as the great blue heron, diving ducks, and dabbling ducks harvest a meal from the windrows of eelgrass left on the beach.

At Grays Harbor, fifty thousand ducks and six thousand brants utilize the eelgrass beds during the winter. Padilla Bay has a winter brant population of five thousand to eight thousand, with over forty-seven thousand stopping to feed during the spring migration. Half the birds on the Pacific migration route (one of four primary flyways in North America—the Pacific, Central, Mississippi, and Atlantic) pass through Padilla Bay.

FORESTED SWAMP

A good place to observe a forested swamp is at the Nisqually Wildlife Refuge on the River Trail. Here the high forest canopy consists primarily of black cottonwood trees with incredibly large, straight trunks. Visible in the understory are the thorny, tan-lacquered canes of salmonberry and the bright red winter stems of red-osier dogwood along with willows and sweet gale, its resin-dotted leaves perfuming the air. In the spring the huge golden flowers of skunk cabbage light up the swamp,

Skunk cabbage

while its 2-foot-long leaves lend the scene a primitive, tropical air.

Dominated by woody plants, forested swamps develop in areas where water saturates the ground—often as a result of overflow from nearby streams or rivers. The ground in a swamp is almost always soggy, and during times of high rainfall and runoff it becomes so saturated that water rises around the roots of the trees and shrubs. Often found on floodplains, forested swamps are an important factor in flood control. They can quickly absorb and slowly release large volumes of water, thus preventing it from moving into the surrounding countryside. Sometimes forested swamps look quite unremarkable, only hinting at the water they can hold in the muck at the base of their roots, but the high-water mark on their stems and trunks gives them away. Because it takes many years to produce the mature trees that characterize them, forested swamps are very difficult to replace.

In Washington forested swamps are most common at lower elevations, especially on the coastal plains and in the glaciated areas near Puget Sound. Some shrub-covered sites began as freshwater marshes and are slowly being invaded by trees. Some forested swamps are dominated by shrubs, such as salmonberry and hardhack, while others are a mix of trees and shrubs. Western red cedar, black cottonwood, red alder, Oregon ash, and bigleaf maple are the dominant trees. The understory includes vine maple, devil's club, hardhack, crab apple, skunk cabbage, and various mosses and ferns.

In the Pacific Northwest the lack of rainfall during the summer months generally favors the development of coniferous forests as opposed to forests of broad-leaved trees. This is because conifers can continue significant photosynthesis throughout the winter, since their leaves are still on the trees, whereas the growth of deciduous trees must take place in a short period of time when there is the presence of a photosynthesizing leaf and inadequate water. Forested swamps are the exception; as collection points for water, these lowlands provide sufficient moisture when sunlight and warmth are at their peak to encourage the growth of hardwood trees, which then coexist with the coniferous western red cedar that, along with skunk cabbage, is the most common member of the swamp community.

With its soft, stringy red bark, scented wood, and graceful boughs, western red cedar is perhaps the Northwest's most easily identified conifer. The leaves of the western red cedar are tiny overlapping scales rather than elongated needles. Lightweight cedar wood contains oils that prevent or slow decay, and it splits evenly and easily. Native Pacific Northwesterners made canoes, ropes, housing, cooking utensils, clothing, and numerous tools from this huge and plentiful species. The demand for cedar shakes has sent people back into the woods to salvage cedar tree parts left there in the first quarter of the century by loggers who considered their value to be marginal—many of these leftovers remain in prime condition. Because it grows very slowly, timber companies see no monetary return for planting this tree and it is not included in reforestation plans.

Often the first tree species to colonize burned, logged, or otherwise disturbed areas, red alder is usually a successional tree in the Pacific Northwest, meaning that it will ultimately be crowded out by more dominant species. In some swamp communities, however, it appears to be a climax species, existing as a dominant member of the forest canopy on a continuing basis. Many people view alder as an undesirable species, even as a weed, but it should be appreciated for its ability to enrich the soil. Nodules on the the roots of alder trees are inhabited by a filamentous bacteria that extracts nitrogen from the atmosphere, where it is normally unavailable for plant use, and converts it to a useable form. By enriching the soil in this way and raining nitrogen-rich leaves into the water, alders provide extra nitrogen in places where it is often in short supply.

Neither of the two dominant tree species, red cedar nor red alder, make a living only in a swamp. Both tolerate a variety of habitats but seldom grow in very dry areas. They both grow well in areas that flood in winter, although red cedar dies after long-term submersion in deep water.

Black cottonwoods grow to great heights—from 100 to 180 feet—in the Pacific Northwest. The high canopy they create moderates the amount of sunlight reaching the forest-swamp floor and reduces the loss of moisture so that although the understory plants must grow in low light they benefit from high humidity. The large, triangular, leathery leaves of the cottonwood are a cool

Great horned owl

green above and silvery beneath and turn brilliant yellow in the fall. Cottonwoods hold an immense amount of water; when cut, water drains from the trunk and the stump, the wood will barely float, and sections of the tree are able to sprout for several years after cutting. All trees and shrubs, but cottonwoods in particular, act as huge spraying devices, taking water from the landscape, moving it up the trunk, and releasing it to the atmosphere through openings in the leaves, thereby cooling the landscape and raising the relative humidity.

Apparently, cottonwood, and Oregon ash, are able tolerate the low oxygen levels found in swamps by moving oxygen down into their root zone at a rate great enough to allow its movement out of the root hairs and into the surrounding oxygen-deficient muck and soil in which they grow. It has been suggested that the brown deposits found around all plant roots in waterlogged soils are evidence of the oxidation of iron and manganese created by the movement of oxygen out of the root into the adjacent oxygen-poor soil.

Skunk cabbage marks the presence of a wetland; it frequents areas where seepage water moves slowly and has a tendency to stagnate. In swamps it appears scattered beneath fans of cedar, a beacon for hordes of flies and beetles, to whom the protein-rich pollen of this massive perennial is a welcome food source. The unusual skunklike odor of this plant is counterbalanced by the elegance of its leaves and blossom. Skunk cabbage contains highly irritating and potentially dangerous calcium oxalate crystals. These crystals also occur in dumbcane (a tropical houseplant), sorrel, and antifreeze. Small quantities cause an excruciating local irritation, and greater amounts can cause permanent kidney and intestinal damage. Boiling the plant detoxifies it and renders it edible. Animals that eat skunk cabbage apparently have a built-in system to cope with the calcium oxalate, although how this works is not known.

Devil's club dominates the undergrowth of forested swamps in the Pacific Northwest. Early explorers wrote of unpleasant encounters with this well-armed species. The stems and dramatic leaves bristle with long thorny spines, and the puncture wounds these produce can become swollen and infected. From a safe distance, devil's club forms a bold green understory; it is especially attractive in late summer and fall when it is decorated with bright red berries.

Devil's club

Most large mammals tend to visit forested swamps rather than live in them, although deer, elk, and bear come to graze on skunk cabbage and other understory species. More usual inhabitants are frogs, salamanders, and small mammals, such as the tiny shrew mole, which measures only 4 inches long. Shrew moles have sensitive, elongated snouts and the shieldlike front feet that identify them as moles. Because their front feet are narrower than those of the larger moles, shrew moles walk, climb, and swim with greater agility. They find swamps to be a plentiful source of food—insects, spiders, and other delectables.

FRESHWATER MARSH

Birds and marshes go together, and the chatter of red-winged blackbirds as they swing on cattails is one of the sweet sounds of the marsh. Cattails interspersed with sedges line the shore and form a backdrop for bright yellow iris and delicate pink water-plantain. The surface of the water is tightly packed with lily pads curled up at the edges and masses of pondweed, an elliptical plant that grows so prolifically the entire water surface is a mosaic of shields.

This wetland type is probably the one most familiar to us. Dominated by grasses and sedges, freshwater marshes vary in size from small potholes to the margins of ponds and lakes to vast acres of squishy ground full of red-winged blackbirds, ducks, and herons. By definition, marshes have a water table permanently above the sediment surface, but unlike the rivers and streams that feed them the water movement within them is slow. Marshes can be categorized as shallow, with large plants growing above the water, or deep, with plants either floating on or submerged beneath the surface. Often dominated by just one species of plant, shallow marshes are lush with bulrushes, reeds, or cattails. The high water prevents smaller plants from creating an understory, making the habitat unfriendly to small mammals.

The depth of the water, the severity of the wave action, and temperature patterns within the body of water all influence which plants and animals live in a particular marsh. Shallow water on a summer day may reach fairly high temperatures if it is not shaded and not disturbed by waves. While these conditions may promote more rapid plant growth, they also mean that less oxygen is held dissolved in the water and available for organisms to breathe.

The height of a marsh's vegetation, the amount of area it covers, and which species are present all influence the resident bird populations. Marshes are attractive to birds because they provide appropriate nest-

Ducks and yellow pond lilies

ing sites and adequate food, which prevents them from wasting energy in foraging over large areas and allows them to build the energy reserves necessary for productive egg laying. Red-winged blackbirds, terns, rails, bitterns, coots, ducks, herons, and geese all use marshes throughout their lives. Like eelgrass beds, marshes play a significant role in bird migration along the Pacific flyway.

One mammal found in freshwater marshes is the beaver. Beavers often contribute to the development of marshes and ponds when they build a dam across a stream. As compensation for an inefficient digestive system beavers consume vast quantities of vegetation. The leaves and bark of deciduous trees such as alder, willow, and cottonwood rank high on the list of foods that beavers favor. During the fall, they poke saplings into the bottom mud of the pond to serve as fresh food throughout the winter. They also eat the roots and stems of the yellow pond lily as well as bracken fern, pondweed, sedges, and cattails.

Muskrats, named for the musky scent exuded by a pair of glands found in their abdomens, also frequent marshes. They feed on the tender roots of aquatic plants and on snails and mussels. Muskrats often live in burrows in lake and stream banks. But sometimes they live with beavers in a beaver lodge or build their own dome-shaped homes of cattails and grasses.

A variety of small rodents live in and around marshes. The Pennsylvania meadow mouse can be found in wet places in the northeast part of Washington, while the Townsend's meadow mouse lives on the western side of the Cascades in both Washington and Oregon. Richardson's water vole forages in creeks feeding into marshes. The Pacific jumping mouse lives along the edges of marshes and tributary streams. The cinereous shrew and the vagrant shrew, both insectivores, live along marsh edges.

Among the invertebrates, annelid worms, mollusks, crustaceans, and insects all are well represented in freshwater marshes. The abundance and distribution of each group vary with the specific habitat. Invertebrates are important members of the community, efficiently converting plant cells to animal protein and playing a significant role in breaking plant material down to manageable size for use by bacteria and fungi.

Thread worms (nematodes) are among the most abundant creatures in the world, usually living as parasites on plants and animals alike. Brownish to white and often only a few millimeters long, nematodes are easily recognized by their nearly continual whiplike thrashing. Segmented worms are commonly found in the debris of stagnant water and in mats of filamentous algae. Tubifex worms are bottom-dwellers—entire stretches of pond floor may be covered with their undulating tubes. With their heads buried in the tubes these worms function like little suction hoses, eating decaying debris and excreting the digested material back out onto the floor of the marsh. Leeches prefer the vegetation of shallow water. The easiest way to find them is to wade around shallow ponds with bare legs. One group of leeches sucks blood primarily from amphibians and waterfowl, while the other group preys on snails, insect larvae, and crustaceans.

Freshwater mollusks live in the soft mud of the marsh or on aquatic vegetation. Small clams are common, but larger clams and mussels are less frequently found. Numerous snails crawl on plants and the detritus on the marsh bottom, rasping algae and diatoms from these surfaces with a radula, a beltlike structure in their mouth that bears tiny teeth. Because they are so abundant, snails and other mollusks serve as staples in the diets of many vertebrates.

Crustaceans inhabit bottom mud, open water, or aquatic vegetation. Crayfish, the largest crustaceans found in freshwater marsh communities, scavenge aggressively. Burrowing in soft muck or hiding under sheltering rocks and logs, crayfish offer an attractive meal for mink, raccoons, and predaceous fish. Fairy shrimp, larger and more mobile than other shrimp, hide in marsh vegetation. (Their large numbers dominate shallow wetlands in cooler seasons and serve as an important food source for fish, amphibians, and birds.) Drifting or free-swimming plankton are also important members of the marsh community.

Although water boatmen, water bugs, backswimmers, and diving beetles spend their entire lives in an aquatic environment, the majority of wetland insects live there only as juveniles. Adult dragonflies, mayflies, damselflies, mosquitoes, and midges all feed in the area, but they do not reenter the water as adults.

Midges sometimes appear in the air above marshes as huge black hordes against the evening sun as they swarm in mating clusters. Their larvae, called bloodworms because of their rich red color, are able to flourish under conditions of extreme oxygen depletion. Since these conditions occur whenever there is an excess of decomposing organic matter, bloodworms are indicators of pollution and an important source of food for frogs, fish, and diving birds. Surface-feeding birds such as swallows, ducks, terns, and small gulls feed the adult midges.

Everyone recognizes the whine of a mosquito as it descends onto a bare arm. Only the charitable accept the attack, knowing that the insect is a female foraging food for her offspring. Mosquitoes are attracted to the carbon dioxide in exhaled breath, often finding their prey by following the trail of the gas to its source. Strong body odors and perfumes also alert mosquitoes to human presence.

Dragonflies are easy to spot as they speed and dart through the marsh area. They mark their territory by constantly patrolling its perimeter and defend its boundaries by attacking intruders. However, in marshes not plagued by insect collectors, the dragons seem almost tame, sometimes resting on a shoulder or hand, although the slightest movement sends them off on patrol. The immature stages of the dragonfly and damselfly are voracious carnivores and efficient hunters that crawl and swim throughout the forests of aquatic leaves and stems.

Water striders skate on dimples, never breaking the water's surface as they skitter about searching for prey. They are true bugs, whose relatives include the predatory backswimmers, with their efficient oarlike legs, and the giant water bugs, which may grow to 3 or 4 inches long. Bugs have beaks, and these efficient devices can pierce rather sturdy body coverings. Giant water bugs capture, hold, and suck out the liquid contents of small fish and large tadpoles. The water boatmen prefer feeding on algae and assorted bottom debris.

Caddis fly larvae, a popular bait among fishermen, have caterpillarlike bodies with filamentous gills along the abdominal segments. To protect their soft, vulnerable bodies, they build portable tubular cases out of small rocks, twigs, sand grains, or even grass stems, which they stack like logs in a cabin. They drag these cases along with them as they shred detritus, scrape algae from rocks, strain edible materials out of the water, or prey on smaller creatures.

Many beetles live in marshes, but two kinds dominate: the predaceous diving beetles and the whirligig beetles, whose twirling produces random patterns on the surface of the water as they feed.

Blue-green algae inhabit both freshwater and saltwater systems. For reasons yet unknown, some of these algae, including *Anabaena* and *Microcystis,* sometimes produce a nervous-system toxin that kills mammals. Another blue-green alga produces swimmer's itch. Some blue-green algae produce a toxin related to that produced by the organism associated with red tides. The trigger that causes these usually benign organisms to produce toxins remains unknown.

SALT MARSH

Salt marshes are horizontal places where great stretches of slightly tilted land drain to the sea. Wind hisses through the grass carrying the pungent odor of salty decay. Swallows skim low, lunching on masses of insects hatching from the marsh, and high up, a hawk circles, watching for a careless rabbit or a snake basking in the sun's warmth. But much of the life here is underwater, where bacteria decompose fallen plant stalks and where tiny snails, only 2 millimeters long, wander around scraping algae off stems. The marsh is a haven from scouring wave action and an undisturbed source of food. Gentle tidal movements create backward flows and wash in cool salt water to mix with the incoming freshwater seepage. With their great sweeps of horizon, unfettered movement of air, and interesting odors, salt marshes are often the best sources of solitude available to humans living near urban settings.

Salt marshes occur near river mouths, in bays, on coastal plains, and around protected lagoons. They are zones of accumulation, places where silt carried down from the headlands collects as the water slows its pace when it meets the inertia of the marsh. The new silty mud constantly shifts around until it is colonized by tiny algae, which secrete a glue that slowly binds the particles together. The stage is set for the invasion of rooted plants, and as they grow out from the land, binding the silt to the substrate, more mud catches in the root hairs and the marsh grows, building a shelf between the eroding headlands and the intertidal area.

This is a world of changing salinity. When little fresh water drains from the headlands, salinity rises and pools of salt water are retained in depressions in the ground. In these lagoons water evaporates, and soon salt crystals are deposited on the edges of the marsh and along the leaves and stalks of plants. As the salinity goes up, fewer plants and animals can tolerate living here. Through the process known as osmosis the salt in the environment acts to pull the water out of plant cells, and as they lose their water, the cells collapse and the plant wilts. Some salt marsh plants have waxy coverings, which, by protecting the openings in the cell walls, prevent this loss of water. Salinity is highest near the shore of the marsh, then gradually decreases as it is diluted with tidal water. This gradation of salinity is often indicated by changing bands of plant species. It is echoed by animal species, with the most salt-tolerant near shore and the least salt-tolerant on the side of tidal water movement.

Glasswort entwined with dodder

Large variations in temperature, along with alternate flooding and exposure of vegetation, influence this community. In the summer when the tide comes in the water warms from contact with the warm mud. Small organisms slide in and feed on roots and stems of marsh plants. The receding tide exposes the marsh to extremely high temperatures in the summer and freezing temperatures in the winter as the ameliorating covering of water disappears. Animals are forced to adjust to these wide temperature extremes by burrowing into the substrate or following the water. The alternate wetting and drying of the soil in salt marshes also slows the rate at which organic matter decomposes; this slowdown results in the process being taken over by bacteria that use sulfur instead of oxygen. The distinctive rotten-egg aroma associated with salt marshes arises from the decay products.

Perennials dominate most salt marshes because salt water and tidal agitation deter the germination of annual seeds and make the establishment of seedlings difficult. Many of the perennials reproduce vegetatively (a part of the plant breaks away from the parent and essentially becomes a new plant). Plants reproduced in this fashion are called clones, and they can be notably long-lived. Marshes with high salinity are often dominated by slough sedge and salt marsh bulrush, while marshes with lower salinity (brackish) are often dominated by seaside arrowgrass or by smooth cordgrass, American threesquare, glasswort, and fleshy jaumea. Other plant inhabitants include dodder, Lyngby's sedge, and seashore saltgrass.

Few large animals are found in salt marshes. Raccoons come to forage; they can often be seen gazing off into space as they pat and sift through the muddy substrate with their nearly prehensile front feet. Beaver and nutria also visit the marshes, although they usually build in the uplands. River otters follow estuarine channels down into the lowlands to collect clams, crayfish, and some fish. Rabbits and mice graze on the leaves and stems of rooted marsh plants, while the harvest mouse lives primarily on their seeds. Deer mice, coots, rails, and several species of ducks consume salt marsh plants as a part of their diet. Spiders, lizards, and shrews prey upon insects. Weasels, snakes, and owls pursue smaller mammals, and marsh hawks collect rabbits and coots. Fox, coyote, opossums, weasels, and striped skunks all forage in salt marshes.

The depth of a marsh's water, how much it is diluted by fresh water, and the accessibility of nesting sites all influence whether birds come to nest and feed. Birds that forage from sediment surface layers along shorelines often move into salt marshes. Dunlins, western sandpipers, sanderlings, and knots appear on exposed beaches in the lower parts of estuaries. Dowitchers and whimbrels occur in inner bays and flats that have greater protection. Waders, such as greater yellowlegs, great blue herons, and egrets, search shallow areas for invertebrates and fish. This habitat also shelters killdeer, song sparrows, and savannah sparrows. The crow, the northern harrier, and the peregrine falcon are found here, along with the common loon and the pied-billed grebe.

Although few birds nest in a salt marsh, many stop here in fall and winter. Often salt marshes are overwintering locations for birds that use the Arctic tundra and interior freshwater marshes for breeding grounds. Among the important overwintering locations in Washington are the Nisqually Delta , the Skagit River Delta, Salt Creek (near Port Angeles), Dungeness Spit, and the American Camp lagoons on San Juan Island.

Salt marshes are an important element in the life cycle of salmon, who pass through these wetlands at least twice in a lifetime: once as juveniles (fry) moving from their river birthplace to the sea and again as adults en route to their spawning grounds. The tidal ecosystems supply a rich food source, and the fish grow fast. With a mortality rate of 59 to 77 percent in juvenile salmon, the early marine period is critical to the species survival. Disturbance of the marsh and estuarine system can be disastrous. In addition to other fish fry, this community also harbors staghorn sculpin and shiner perch.

Insects do not display physiological adaptations to high salt levels. Instead, they leave when the marsh floods and return to graze as the waters recede. Leafhoppers, aphids, and grasshoppers all graze on marsh plants. Snails, amphipods, hermit crabs, snapping shrimp, sand fleas, pillbugs, crabs, periwinkles, mussels, and immature insects feed on the algae and detritus, releasing and using the energy stored in the plant tissue. Mosquitoes find salt marshes a particularly favorable place to breed. The mud harbors ghost shrimp, bacteria, and fungi.

Many distinctive habitats exist within salt marshes, each with definite growing conditions and therefore unique species. At least ten discrete microhabitats have been described within marshes. The presence of these microhabitats, such as creeks and drainage channels that allow greater penetration of the tidal waters, is one characteristic of a fully developed salt marsh. The rich variety of microhabitats found in marshes occupy relatively narrow belts but have extensive boundaries next to other systems. Transitional habitats, with their numerous species, increase dramatically. Although few species may live in the marsh itself, the entire area affected by the marsh often has many different species and extensive community complexity.

WET MEADOW

Low-lying ground becomes a wet meadow when it collects runoff from higher areas. A wet meadow is often an intermediate stage, connecting perennially wet ground, a marsh or swamp, and ground that is just high enough to exclude water. Often underlain by layers of clay or other impermeable materials, wet meadows have poor drainage. In the summer months, the soil may simply be waterlogged, but during the non-growing, rainy season standing water is visible on the surface.

A typical example of a wet meadow is a pasture that receives drainage from surrounding hills and passes it on to ditches or streams at a yet lower elevation. The clear markers for wet meadows are the tufts of the soft-stemmed bulrush. Often called tule or simply bulrush, the soft-stemmed bulrush grows with reed canarygrass, forget-me-nots, monkeyflower, buttercups, and other rushes and sedges. Although cows may trample

Rush and dragonfly

and graze wet meadows, they apparently find the bulrush unpalatable.

Wet meadows sometimes pass through a successional stage in which shrubs and trees invade the area. Woody species such as red-osier dogwood, willows, ninebark, and hardhack, although they also grow in drier situations, are tolerant of low levels of soil saturation, and for reasons that are not entirely clear they sometimes move into a wet meadow, as do red alder, cottonwood, and quaking aspen.

A unique set of conditions influences the formation of wet meadows above 3,500 feet. Timberline, the upper limit of tree occurrence, occupies an uneven line in the mountains but usually ends around 5,300 feet. Naturally, this varies with latitude and the direction the slope faces, the line dropping lower on cool northern exposures and rising higher on warmer southern faces. In the Cascades, this variation creates a subalpine meadow-forest mosaic, in which the appearance of montane meadow communities correlates strongly with how long the snow lasts. As the snows begin to melt, snowbed communities emerge. Some plants break through the snow crust to bloom immediately; others unfold slowly. The species most typical of the snowbed community is black alpine sedge, which forms a short, dense mat. Other early plants include steer's head, turkey-pea, and the photogenic glacier lily. Later in the season, wet meadow species will replace this association of short-lived plants.

The montane environment is a particularly stressful one. Frozen for much of the year, water is largely unavailable. Low temperatures create a very short summer growing season, during which strong sunlight and drying breezes pull the available water out of the plant and into the air. These factors, plus the availability of nutrients, influence the mixture of plants found in a montane wetland community.

Sitka valerian and green false hellebore are the dominant species found on steep, moist slopes that are plagued by avalanches. They survive because they overwinter in underground parts, and thus the scouring action of fast-moving snow removes only a year of greenery. Often reaching heights of 4 to 6 feet, this lush montane community provides a near-tropical experience. In areas where slightly more water is available, species such as the showy yellow monkeyflowers, especially Lewis's and subalpine monkeyflowers, grow along with coltsfoot (also found down to sea level) fringed grass-of-parnassus, and marsh marigold. Typical tree species include subalpine fir and mountain hemlock.

Animals frequenting montane wet meadows include picas, marmots, mountain goats and sheep, bear, elk, and birds. The larger animals tend to pass through and move to lower forested areas in the winter. Many of the smaller animals hibernate after a summer of intensive grazing, which helps to maintain the meadow's trimmed appearance.

The tailed frog is a distinctive amphibian found in montane environments and belongs to the bell toad family. A throwback to its more primitive ancestors, this frog has such uncommon characteristics as ribs, nine vertebrae instead of eight, unusually shaped vertebrae, and numerous chromosomes instead of few. Restricted to the Pacific Northwest, one genus of tailed frogs occurs from northwestern California to western Montana. The only other close relatives of these tailed frogs live in New Zealand.

Like many other wetland communities and all alpine communities, montane wetlands are fragile places, easily damaged and slow to recover.

Glacier lilies in a montane wet meadow

They are particularly susceptible to heavy foot traffic, which not only destroys plant cover but also cuts into the thin layer of soil and initiates erosion patterns. Montane wetlands are easily loved to death.

HISTORY OF HUMAN INTERACTION _____

Lowlands have been drained throughout human history as people needed more room and fertile land to grow crops and pasture farm animals. As people moved into these areas, times of high water and flooding have threatened their safety. Wetlands store and slow the flow of runoff water and protect those living downstream from floods. The floods that occurred in 1993 along the Mississippi River are good examples of the consequences of trying to exclude water from its natural flood plain. As extensive as this huge river's remaining wetlands are, it became clear that there weren't enough wetlands available to absorb the volumes of water traveling down its path. To create more agricultural land, we have tried to confine bodies of water that, in the tradition of the Nile and all other major river systems, annually surge over their banks and blanket the surrounding land with a fresh layer of soil. Although farmers might welcome the layer of fertile soil on their land, it adds little to their living rooms.

Humans have long used marshes for grazing sheep and other livestock and for haying, as on the East Coast. Many people consider filling or draining salt marshes and other wetlands to be their best and highest use. Only recently has the value of these abused and rapidly disappearing resources been recognized. In addition to their high productivity—which we enjoy as tasty fish, crab, and shellfish—marshes are important in flood and erosion control. Salt marshes also provide aesthetic and recreational amenities, including bird-watching, hiking, fishing, and hunting. Thousands of birds nest in, feed in, or migrate through wetlands. That wetlands are frequently close to major population centers and are easily accessible for human enjoyment is a danger to these vulnerable systems.

The development of coastal areas has modified bird populations in the Pacific Northwest. Surveys done from the 1940s to 1981 show that migrating brant declined by 74 percent in Washington, by 90 percent in Oregon, and by 98 percent in California. Apparently they went to Mexico, where migrating brant populations have gone from 80,000 in the early 1950s to 130,000 in the mid-1980s. The expansion of human activity has had its impact. We build more marinas, drain more marshes, and do more boating than we did in the past. It is clear that a vast population of birds utilizes the eelgrass beds of the Pacific Northwest and that the continued destruction of eelgrass beds would have a massive impact on our bird populations.

Salmon have a long and important history in the cultural and religious traditions of Northwest native peoples. They are a valuable and currently endangered resource, and controversy surrounds their environmental, economic, and cultural relationships. The high-volume, rapid-flow rivers have been dammed, to the detriment of spawning fish populations. Extensive road building associated with logging further degrades the clarity and oxygen capacity of our streams. Clear-cuts remove all vegetation and root systems, sending soil cascading down hillsides into streams and rivers. Logging equipment breaks up the streambed and adds to the silt load, which clogs the gills of fish and prevents them from breathing. The addition of excessive organic matter to streams in logged areas increases decomposition, and the oxygen in the stream becomes depleted and unavailable to fish. As vegetation is stripped from stream edges, the water temperature rises and salmon find these higher temperatures (and lower oxygen levels) unlivable, contributing to the continued decline of salmon runs.

Throughout the world, eelgrass beds stabilize bottom sediments and provide food and habitat for marine inhabitants. Such beds demonstrate their value when humans destroy them through dredging, sewage discharge, oil pollution, and heavy plankton blooms. Scallops, fish, clams, and crabs disappear with the removal of eelgrass meadows. In Europe, brant geese numbers declined severely when eelgrass beds were unavailable for food and shelter. In England, the experimental removal of an eelgrass bed resulted in the immediate reduction, by erosion, of a sand bank by 12 inches. In Chesapeake Bay, eelgrass removal resulted in the loss of many filter-feeding invertebrates and several flatfish, in addition to 8 inches of sediment. A single storm caused all this damage. No erosion occurred in an adjacent undisturbed bed.

Wetlands are increasingly being considered as a way to provide treatment for wastewater sources. Their ability to remove nutrients and suspended materials from sewage and storm runoff makes them an attractive option to more costly treatment systems. Since this function could include the channeling of pollutants including heavy metals into the wetlands, more information is needed about the fate of these pollutants, and such data are scarce at the present time. Studies done at the Puyallup Research and Extension Center on nonwetland soil suggest that heavy metals applied to soil through sewage sludge do not move even 6 inches in the soil but remain bound to soil particles in the sludge.

In the southeastern states, tidal marsh wetlands are being used as a third-level treatment system for wastewater. Very few cities have gone to the third level of treatment because of the expense of conventional systems. Tertiary treatment returns water to the environment in a clean, drinkable condition. Although not tertiary in effect, marsh systems *are* able to remove many microorganisms, growth-promoting elements, and suspended solids, the residue from secondary waste treatment plants.

The University of Florida passed secondarily treated municipal sewage through a bed of water hyacinths—plants that have aggressively choked many of Florida's waterways—and out into a cypress swamp. Nitrogen and phosphorus encourage excessive plant growth and entangling mats of algae downstream, but this treatment removed nearly all of the nitrogen and phosphorus,

Coltsfoot in bloom

as well as many viruses and bacteria. Suspended solids, tiny particles not heavy enough to immediately drop to the bottom, were greatly reduced. The laboratory culture of coliform bacteria, found in the gut of all mammals and some other vertebrates, is used as an indicator of fecal pollution. In these test sites, the bacterial counts dropped by a factor of 150. Trees growing in this treatment area grew over two and a half times faster than those not in the third-level treatment area. The experiments were highly successful.

In a similar venture, the Disney World complex in Orlando, Florida, uses water hyacinths to provide recyclable water for the park. A water hyacinth pond takes 5 days to treat wastewater, whereas a conventional municipal treatment plant takes 6 hours. But when costs are compared, the pond system is clearly much less expensive.

The Pacific Northwest is beginning to examine water treatment alternatives. The city of Yelm is embarking on a pioneering project as it attempts to use a combination of constructed and natural wetlands to treat its wastewater. This process will produce water that is potable, although its projected use is for irrigation. Such treatment will significantly improve the quality of water being returned to the Nisqually River.

Although hunting and fishing involve thousands of people every year, more and more people spend time in wetlands in nonconsumptive ways, watching and photographing wildlife and plants, and kayaking and canoeing. Wetland sites are yielding cultural artifacts from Native American settlements. Schools have found students receptive to these areas as interesting places to study interactive ecological systems. Wetlands are used for nature study, for literary work, for art, for research, for education, and for sightseeing. It is difficult to quantify these kinds of uses, and the common practice of counting heads is an insignificant measure of such complex pleasures.

Wetlands have traditionally been seen as sources of new land or as areas to manage for waterfowl. Over half of the wetlands that existed at the time of European settlement in the United States have been drained, cleared, or filled. Between the 1950s and the 1970s, 11 million acres of wetlands were erased in the United States. Unfortunately, this practice still goes on at the rate of 450,000 acres a year. By the mid-1970s, of the original 215 million acres of wetlands in the lower 48 states, only 46 percent (99 million acres) remained. As a consequence of growing public concern, federal legislation has addressed the issue of wetland loss, preservation, and restoration.

LEGISLATION AND REGULATION

The federal government has mandated no net loss of wetlands. The protection of wetlands comes under the jurisdiction of several federal and state agencies. Under the Clean Water Act, the U.S. Environmental Protection Agency (EPA) has final responsibility for defining wetlands. Guidelines produced by EPA direct the activities of the U.S. Army Corps of Engineers. Another involved agency, the U.S. Fish and Wildlife Service, adopted a definition of wetlands that the Washington State Department of Ecology also uses:

"Wetlands are lands transitional between terrestrial and aquatic systems where the water table is usually at or near the surface, or the land is covered by shallow water. Wetlands must have one or more of the following three attributes:

1. at least periodically, the land supports predominantly hydrophytes,
2. the substrate is predominantly undrained hydric soil,
3. the substrate is non-soil and is saturated with water or covered by shallow water at some time during the growing season of each year."

All water in the state belongs to the people of the State of Washington, regardless of where it resides, and this fact, along with EPA regulations, specifies treatment of wetlands:

■ Wetlands are not to be polluted and are not to be used for domestic waste disposal.
■ Waterfowl and shorebirds are not to have their nesting, feeding, and breeding sites decreased through the modification or destruction of wetlands.
■ Water flows and flood storage capacities should not be blocked through municipal activities.
■ The nutrient exchanges necessary for the livelihood of small fish and the many other forms of wildlife dependent on wetlands are not to be destroyed.
■ Cattle and other livestock are not to defecate in streams and trample stream edges.

Canada goose

The Department of Ecology (DOE) is charged with keeping wetlands available for recreational and aesthetic activities, such as birdwatching, boating, hiking, photography, and fishing. With such a long list of requirements for the DOE to negotiate with local governments, it is no wonder that conflicts often arise.

As a result of this legislation, the U.S. Fish and Wildlife Service has attempted the restoration of 55,000 acres of wetlands on agricultural acreage. Before the 1970s, agriculture was the primary force in accounting for an 87-percent loss of the nation's wetlands. But between the 1970s and the mid-1980s, this figure had dropped to 54 percent. Of course, there are now fewer wetlands to lose. The United States Geologic Survey analyzed eleven estuaries in Puget Sound and determined that 100 percent of the Puyallup River wetlands, 99 percent of the Duwamish River wetlands, and 96 percent of the Samish River wetlands have been lost. The counties with the highest losses were Thurston, with a 55-percent loss; Pierce, with an 82-percent loss; and King, with a 70-percent loss. A Department of Ecology study of wetland losses found a conservative estimate to be 530 acres a year. Many small wetland losses add up to major habitat eradication for wetland plants and animals.

EFFORTS AT MITIGATION

Mitigation is the practice of creating (or setting aside) wetlands to compensate for those that will be destroyed. The Pacific Northwest is a newcomer to the field of wetland mitigation. Wetlands are complex systems, and wetland creators often settle for the appearance of what may become a wetland after many years. Wetland creation requires an understanding of the water characteristics of the new site, as well as the biology of the plants being transplanted and their interrelationships with animal species. Adjacent land use, soil types, topography, site history, sedimentation, hydrology, and the presence of existing wetlands and wildlife all must be factored into the finished product. Because of habitat degradation and loss, more and more attempts will be made to create new wetlands, and with clearly defined goals and adequate monitoring, the success rate may increase.

One example of wetland restoration is a project at the Lincoln Street marsh (Gog-Le-Hi-Te is the Native American name descriptive of the location) in Puyallup. Here a 10-acre industrial fill wetland-upland site was converted to a mud flat with tidal channels, salt marsh, grassland, and shrub land. Habitat was created for juvenile salmonids, waterfowl, shorebirds, raptors, and small mammals. Because of contaminants, much of the original substrate was removed. There are concerns about the remaining substrate materials and about siltation at the wetland entrance affecting tidal exchange water flow through the wetland.

Another project can be seen from Highway 512 going southwest between Puyallup and Interstate 5. A low meadow has been scooped out and soil bulldozed into islands. Stumps have been scattered and dead trees erected. This has created a complex of ponds and shallows that are filling with water and vegetation.

Wetland creation and restoration as mitigation for wetland loss is not a clear success. Often an assumption was made that once a water-holding basin was created and plants were installed, the appropriate wildlife would move into the area and make it whole. Frequently this has not been the case. Sites tend to be too small, and monitoring respon-

Salt marsh at Padilla Bay

sibilities are terminated before the success or failure of the system can be determined.

Several recommendations have accumulated from past Pacific Coast mitigation experiences. Sites smaller than 5 acres may not be viable. The permitting process should be specific about the precise kind of habitat to be created, with design objectives clearly delineated. There should be a sound evaluation of the wetland site to be lost and how comparable elements will be included in the mitigation. After the creation of the new wetland, there should be long-term monitoring and a standard procedure of evaluation of the success of the new wetland. Native species should be used instead of allowing commercial cultivars to replace natives. Sites should be planted when adequate natural precipitation will maintain the vegetation, generally in the fall. Existing wildlife and fish must be protected during construction. Since migratory waterfowl populate wetlands most heavily during the spring and fall and juvenile fish are found there during the spring and summer, these behaviors must be factored into construction plans.

MAINTAINING THE FUTURE

Wetlands enhance the quality of our water and the quality of our lives. We use them as places to learn, to photograph, to hunt, and to fulfill those ineffable human desires for stillness and beauty. Unfortunately, these lovely environments are destroyed by our voracious appetite for land. Island County is protecting its wetlands by adding a conservation futures tax to property taxes. This money goes toward purchasing development rights to property currently being used or adding to open space in the community. By using a preserved wetland as the centerpiece of a development, one community in Island County has emphasized both the practicality of preservation and the pleasure of living near a wetland.

In spite of the many ways we have found to destroy wetlands, there are ways we can each help maintain a healthy wetland system. We need to work with county and state governments to provide tax relief for owners of wetlands, so that wetlands can be maintained and preserved. We need to make sure that school districts include activities related to wetlands in their curriculum. We need to examine roadside spraying programs to see if they are really necessary—many compounds from the herbicides and pesticides sprayed along our roads eventually end up in our wetlands and finally in our water. Most forestry practices include extensive application of sprays, and these too move downstream to collect in wetlands. We should examine land-use management plans carefully to determine the necessity of further businesses, malls, and road paving.

Kingfisher

As more and more land is sealed off from water absorption, additional stresses are placed on the remaining wetlands to sponge up peak water flows. Watershed logging practices should be reviewed to determine their long-term value. Clear-cutting practices should be revised. Scraping away every tree and shrub because it makes logging easier and cheaper should not be tolerated. With little vegetation to brake the water's flow, soil is carried away, gullies are cut, root systems of remaining plants have difficulty maintaining their upright position, and downstream wetlands are clogged with silt. Channel and port dredging disturb shallow harbor wetlands, clouding the water with mud and soil particles and destroying habitat for young fish. Boaters contribute oil to the water surface; much of this pollution could be prevented with more careful handling of lubricants and fuels. Agricultural applications of herbicides and pesticides could be reduced with more ecologically sound farming methods. Livestock need to be fenced off from wetlands, both to prevent trampling and to prevent water pollution with animal fecal material. We need to think beyond our short-term, personal goals and look down a corridor of time where the consequences of our actions affect our lives. With commitment and planning, we can learn to live with the land and allow it to function in such a way that all of our lives are enhanced.

We compile lists of reasons for coexisting with wetlands, for maintaining them, for enhancing them, as if we need to justify their importance in our lives. Perhaps our need to justify is symptomatic of an unease deep in our unconscious that tells us we should not tinker with that about which we are so ignorant. Wetlands carry a geologic history far longer than our own and, regardless of the headlong drive to fill and pave all of them, will probably exist well beyond our tenure on this planet. Wetlands are a functioning part of the natural world; their interactions and complexities are infinitely wondrous; we should let them be.

Milkweed at McNary National Wildlife Refuge

2
TWENTY-FIVE WALKS
AND PADDLES

Freshwater Marsh

TWENTY-FIVE WALKS AND PADDLES

1

ARBORETUM WATERFRONT TRAIL

Community: Freshwater marsh, forested swamp
Size: Wetland, about 15 acres
Ownership: University of Washington
Season: Open all year
Cautions: No jogging, no bicycling
Facilities: Interpretive trail guide
Fee: None, unless parking on campus
Hours: Parking lots closed between 11:00 P.M. and 6:00 A.M.
Maps: Local
Highlights: Marsh and swamp plants, floating walkways, views
Nearest Town: Seattle

From Seattle, take I-5 to Highway 520 and go east in the direction of the Evergreen Point Floating Bridge and Bellevue; take the Arboretum exit and at the stop light, continue across Montlake Boulevard onto Lake Washington Boulevard. An immediate left turn leads to the entrance of the Broadmoor Golf Club. Park in the lot to the left of this entrance. If you miss the left turn, circle through the Arboretum and after looping past the headquarters, go down the hill and park at the end of the drive, just outside the Broadmoor Golf Club. From the parking lot take the trail to the right and follow it to the entrance of Foster Island. The other end of the trail is at the Museum of History and Industry; park in the lower lot.

Traffic thunders overhead on the Evergreen Point Floating Bridge and the drone and sputter of boat engines echo across the water. In the midst of incessant activity, this wetland trail offers both a green moment of peace and a textbook illustration of our influence on the natural world. The installation of a floating walkway connecting Foster Island and other small bits of land to the Arboretum allows the walker to experience various views of the lake and of the vegetation. This is a collection of both native and nonnative plants, all blending into an exuberant mass exploiting limited growth space. Those beautiful white water lilies are native to eastern North America, and, unfortunately, they have eliminated the

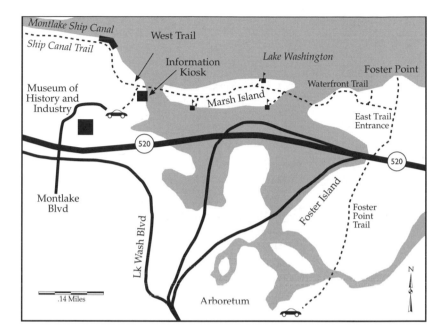

native yellow water lily. The masses of tall purple-flowered plants are purple loosestrife, an aggressive European import that crowds out native plants and grows into thick, impenetrable stands. Local birds and wetland animals do not find it edible or useful as nesting material or nesting habitat. European birch pops up through the less aquatic areas and is joined by reed grass, another East Coast import.

In spite of these reminders of human tampering (often inadvertent), this green, humid wetland is alive with birds and waterfowl. Spongy paths and floating boardwalks hook Foster Island and tiny Marsh Island to the mainland. Cattails and yellow iris (another introduced species but a less invasive one) crowd the shore edges. Hummocks of sphagnum moss form at the bases of tangled willows. Swamp birch and hardhack stand on slightly drier areas, where they are able to fight off the invasion of the water-loving loosestrife. At least five species of willows grow here; the yellow-stemmed Pacific willow has graceful, narrow leaves, and the roots sucker vigorously, producing thick stands of this shrubby tree.

Side trails branch off to observation platforms, sometimes providing new plant discoveries. Occasional stands of horsetail spring up among the roots of willows and birches. Wiry stems with grooves produce a whorl of green wires in umbrella-like forms. These ancient plants once had relatives that grew to 40 feet during the Carboniferous period. Now reaching an average height of 2 feet, they send out underground stems that branch and produce aerial shoots. Horsetail's high silica content made it useful as a scouring pad for early settlers, while miners used it as an assay plant for gold. Its tolerance for heavy metals can be seen in its extensive growth around the old copper smelter site in Tacoma.

Marsh wrens dart through the tangles of brush, often coming quite close to motionless observers. The edge of the marsh might reveal a Virginia rail, a green heron, or a bittern. The pied-billed grebe and American coot paddle along the edges along with numerous mallards and Canada geese. It's about a mile from the Broadmoor parking lot to the Museum of History and Industry parking lot. An hour will take you down each side shoot of a trail and from one end to the other; if walking west, one can continue on with the ship canal path. The Arboretum lies ahead for those walking east. Across the lake is the Montlake fill, the favored site for Seattle bird-watching.

Nonnative water lilies and purple loosestrife

Other Lake Washington wetlands include the Lake Hills greenbelt park in Bellevue, a 3-mile round trip between two marshy lakes, and past slough and blueberry farms, community gardens, and a butterfly garden. Interpretive pamphlets are available from a ranger station on SE 16th Street. In Kirkland, 110 acres of what was formerly a golf course and a frog-legs farm is now called Juanita Bay Park. Two boardwalks extend into the marshy edges of Juanita Bay where there are numerous ducks, turtles, pond lilies, and cattails. A new promenade causeway crosses the edge of the bay, where Forbes Creek, one of the few remaining fish-spawning streams, enters Lake Washington. And in Kent, the Soos Creek County Park covers a 9-mile round-trip trail frequented by bikers along a creek through swampy forest, wet meadows, and hardhack thickets.

2

BELJICA MEADOWS

Community: Wet meadow
Size: 50 acres
Ownership: Glacier View Wilderness, U.S. Department of
    Agriculture, Forest Service
Season: July through October
Cautions: Foot or horse travel only; mosquitoes
Facilities: None
Fee: None
Hours: Always open
Maps: Green Trails, Mount Rainier West 267
Highlights: Flowers
Nearest Town: Ashford

From Elbe take Highway 706 east toward the Nisqually entrance of Mount Rainier National Park, go 3 miles past Ashford and turn left on Copper Creek Road (Forest Road 59). Go 9 miles to reach the Glacier View trailhead. A short trail climbs to intersect trail no. 267; go left for Glacier View, right for Beljica Meadows, Goat Lake, and Lake Christine. The trail winds through dry forest with an understory dominated by beargrass and white rhododendron for about 0.25 mile before descending to Beljica Meadows.

Be prepared for swarms of hungry mosquitoes. Repellent has some slight effect, but wear long sleeves and long pants and plan to make your stops short. The good news is that the meadow trail is about a mile long,

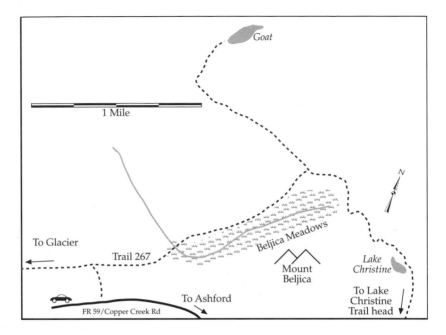

so even with constant walking there are many opportunities to see the variety of subalpine plants that thrive here so briefly each year. Both the mosquitoes and the flowers thrive because of the available water in the meadows. Melting snow provides a constant trickle and rush of stream moving down the slope, catching to pool in depressions in rock and shallow soil.

The floor of this little valley lies at an elevation of 4,480 feet. Wandering through the meadow is a tiny creek that begins near the base of Mount Beljica and flows into the Puyallup River. The creek occasionally widens into shallow pools, not quite ponds, and the whole valley floor is a soggy, wet meadow. A few straggly subalpine fir dot the area, but sedges and forbs dominate the landscape.

Look for the shining white orchid and the bright purple shooting star, a plant related to the handsome houseplant cyclamen. Brilliant Indian paintbrush and lupine are abundant throughout; the careful observer will find, mixed among them, the less spectacular but jaunty elephant's head lousewort. All of the typical mountain meadow flowers are here; asters, bistort, and sharp-edged sedges scatter and mix with the flowers. Beargrass lines the drier edges on the upland side of the trail, and avalanche lilies crowd wet slopes still melting out in July.

At about 1 mile the trail "Ts," and a decision must be made; to the right, in 1 mile is Lake Christine and a chance to scramble up Mount Beljica to a height of 5,478 feet for a magnificent view of Rainier. To the left, in about 1.5 miles, is Goat Lake.

By late August the mosquitoes have subsided and the flower show has changed as the plants hurry to set seed and store starch for overwintering. The orchids and shooting stars are long past, but lupine and Indian paintbrush are still in action, and the silky seed heads of the anemone (pasque flower) are much in evidence. You can find the same flower show in the moist, lush meadows at Paradise, but there you will have to share the trail with chattering crowds, baby strollers, and the roar of arriving tour buses.

Racoon

Beargrass and subalpine fir at Beljica Meadows

3

CHEHALIS WILDLIFE AREA

Community: Freshwater marsh, forested swamps
Overall Size: 800 acres
Ownership: U.S. Department of the Interior, Fish and
  Wildlife Service
Season: Open all year
Cautions: Open to hunting
Facilities: Parking, unmaintained latrine
Fee: None
Hours: Always open
Maps: Available from Fish and Wildlife Service
Highlights: Tremendous variety of birds and wetland vegetation
Nearest Town: Elma

To find the Chehalis Wildlife Refuge, follow Highway 8 (Ocean Beaches) out of Olympia. Several miles east of Elma, Highway 8 becomes Highway 12. Continue on Highway 12 West, and approximately 2 miles before Elma, turn south on Schouweiler Road. The road curves past a gravel company and runs into a Ducks Unlimited parking lot; on any ordinary spring or summer day, follow the road down into the trees and park a little closer to the marsh, especially if toting a canoe or kayak. This land was purchased largely with funds from Ducks Unlimited. Unless you are a duck-hunting enthusiast yourself, avoid this charming wetland in fall and winter but visit often in spring and summer.

To the right, as you pass through a large cyclone gate, are several deep ponds formed in old gravel pits. Fish are purported to be present. Walk down a gravel/rock railroad bed and enjoy the wild roses, red-osier dogwood, hardhack, willows, and in spring, the powerful sweet scent of cottonwood. Then circle back north. Pass under a good-sized bigleaf maple and enter the main wetland. Within a few yards is a large pond on the right. Here is the place to slip in with a boat and make your way quietly through the mint, polygonum, and forget-me-nots out to open water. Watch for wood ducks, cinnamon teal, and green heron.

If boatless, follow the road for perhaps 0.3 mile. Take your time and watch both sides since you are surrounded by swamp and marsh. Watch for a belted kingfisher perched on a branch of a snag, then wade through water on the road skirting small beaver dams, evidently designed to bring up the water level in the swamp. Nutria are known to inhabit the

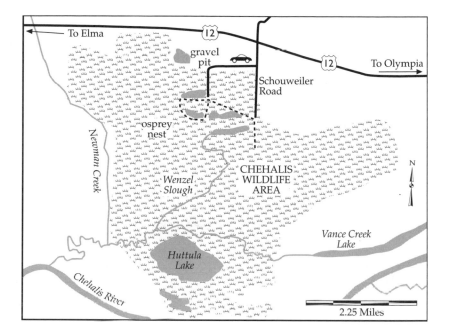

area, and early-morning visitors will almost certainly spot deer and coyote. The occasional elk wanders through, and frogs yelp and plop as the
walker sloshes by. The variety of vegetation is amazing: in a few square
feet are water-plantain springing up from the mud, as well as pond lilies, cattails, rushes, sedges, and pennywort.

At a fork in the road, go to the right through thick old pasture grass.
At the far west end of the wetland is a snaggly old Douglas-fir with an
osprey nest planted squarely on top. You can, if time allows, continue
through the grass, circling through Wenzel Slough, to get a closer look
at the nest. If pressed, turn back and take the left fork. It too passes
through thick pasture grass and finally dead-ends at an old borrow pit,
surrounded by low mucky land with an exciting variety of plants, and
a peaceful little pond. Dragonflies and damselflies hum in the warm
sunlight, red-winged blackbirds call "oaklee" in the distance, and the
highway seems a thousand miles away. For a reminder, though, look to
the north and see the towers of the Satsop Power Station almost within
throwing distance.

The south edge of the wildlife area is bounded by a barbed wire fence,
and there is a strip of land between the wildlife area and the Chehalis
River. Ducks Unlimited and the state are trying to buy this land to complete what is already a delightful and accessible wetland.

Yellow pond lilies at Chehalis Wildlife Area

4

DOSEWALLIPS STATE PARK

Community: Salt marsh
Size: 425 acres
Ownership: Washington State Parks Department
Season: Open all year
Cautions: Read shellfish contamination sign carefully; be prepared
    for mud trail
Facilities: 153 campsites, group camp, rest rooms, showers,
    hookups, hiking trails
Fee: Day use is free; overnight camping fee
Hours: Always open
Maps: Local
Highlights: Bird-watching, seals and sea lions, elk

To reach the park, turn off I-5 at Olympia and take Highway 101 North
for about 60 miles to Dosewallips State Park. Turn right into the park-

ing area marked for beach access and day use. Following the signs for beach access, walk through the campground and cross the bridge over the Dosewallips River. The trail to the beach is immediately to the right and is clearly posted. The Dosewallips River originates high on Mount Anderson, in the eastern Olympic Mountains, and falls steeply to the mile-wide alluvial plain at Brinnon. Here the river slows and mixes with salt water to create an estuary.

The trail starts in a moist forest dominated by huge bigleaf maple, alder, cottonwood, and cedar, with a lush, tangled understory of elderberry, thimbleberry, salmonberry, and the nonnative Himalayan blackberry. After approximately 0.1 mile, the way opens into an old farm field with gnarled apple trees, Canada thistle, berry bushes, and a lovely high hedge of wild roses. Bird calls are a constant background noise.

A thriving population of harbor seals lives here—sometimes so numerous that some of the shellfish beds are contaminated by seal feces. The seals swim up into the sloughs and the river to catch fish, then rest and sun themselves in the shallows. They have created such a problem in the area that the Park Service has erected a fence around Slough no. 1 and tried to entice the seals away by installing a seal float near the mouth

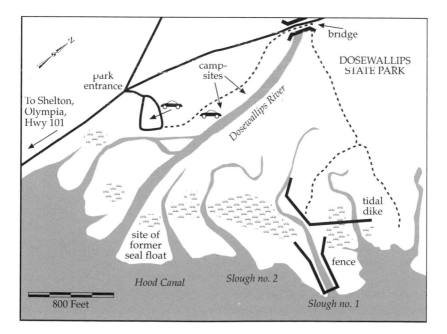

of the river. Although the seals liked this condo, sea lions liked it better, and their massive size quelled all argument; the seals were doomed to whining around the edges. The nightly grunts and roars of sea lion parties created a noise problem for human neighbors, and the Park Service hauled out the float, hoping to discourage this sea lion behavior. This is a great place to watch these marine mammals, but don't eat the shellfish.

From a signboard at a trail junction, two trails move out into high salt marsh vegetation—round-stemmed rushes; glasswort, with its succulent, edible stems; the tall, sticky gumplant; and a number of grass species. The paths all too soon degenerate into mucky trails, and from here on, the hike is more of a wander—pick your way over and around the muddy fingers of the sloughs.

The high tide line is clearly marked with scattered driftwood, dried seaweed, and tiny dried crabs. The vegetation now consists mainly of stiff, spiky saltgrass and glasswort, some of which is wrapped in tangled golden threads of dodder, a parasitic plant. Dodder has no chlorophyll and is incapable of making its own food. Instead it sends fast-growing protrusions into the body of the glasswort and absorbs energy. Both continue to thrive.

Mixed in with the glasswort is another succulent, with small thick leaves and tiny yellow daisylike flowers. This attractive little plant goes by the somewhat grotesque name of fleshy jaumea. More open ground supports goosefoot (*Atriplex*), named at a time when people recognized the shape of a goose's foot.

The way opens to the mud flats and a cobbled beach, which is quite extensive at low tide. Here it is safe to collect clams and oysters. It is also an excellent spot for bird-watching. Watch for raccoon tracks and notice the giant turkey vultures coasting and circling overhead, undisturbed by the occasional attacking crow.

Wander back from the beach through the upper marsh vegetation near Slough no. 2. It is brushier, with a lot of wild rose bushes, triangular-stemmed sedges, and a lovely fernlike plant called silverweed. A member of the rose family, silverweed has leaves that are bright green on the upper side and silver beneath; the flower stalk supports five-petalled yellow flowers.

In the upper sloughs and along the river itself, seasonal flocks of sleek gray cedar waxwings with neatly tailored black masks flit through the bushes. They are especially fond of crab apples and the fruit of mountain ash. They often gorge themselves on the fruit, which ferments in their crop, until they are unable to fly and flop drunkenly through the shrubbery. The great blue heron is also common here, fishing in the shoals. Loons, gulls, and other waterfowl can be seen in the sloughs. In July, elk families are common here as well.

Along Hood Canal, from south to north, the Hamma Hamma, Duckabush, and Dosewallips Rivers all form these lovely sloughs where the rivers slow for the last brief meander before joining the canal. The Dosewallips has the widest estuary but suffers from overuse because of the campground.

Salt marsh at Dosewallips State Park

5

GRAYS HARBOR NATIONAL WILDLIFE REFUGE
Bowerman Basin

Community: Salt marsh, eelgrass beds
Size: 1,500 acres
Ownership: U.S. Department of the Interior, Fish and Wildlife
Service
Season: Open all year, but mainly of interest from mid-April
to mid-May
Cautions: No camping, no firearms, no pets; prepare for wet feet
Facilities: Parking, toilets in April and May, marked trail
Fee: None
Hours: Daylight
Maps: Local
Highlights: Migrating shorebirds
Nearest Town: Hoquiam

From Aberdeen follow Highway 101 through Hoquiam and turn left
onto Highway 109 toward Ocean Shores. At approximately 1 mile turn
left on Paulson Road; then right on Airport Way. The Grays Harbor Natural Wildlife Refuge is closed most of the time; for information out of season, call the Nisqually Wildlife Refuge.

Stalks of spore-bearing horsetail

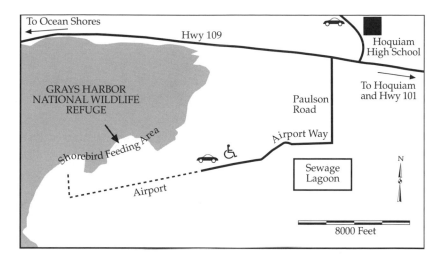

For the best bird viewing walk to the west, and follow the trail signs. Be prepared for mud and wet feet.

Stop at this mud flat in late April and early May and you will find tens of thousands of shorebirds feeding up for their northward migration. This annual feeding frenzy is an obvious and emphatic remainder of the importance of wetlands; 50 percent of the migrating shorebirds on the Pacific flyway use this area. Bowerman Basin is one of only four staging areas in the western United States where migrating birds gather and feed during migration. The other staging areas are Humboldt and San Francisco Bays in California and Willapa Bay here in Washington.

Plan to arrive at high tide, when the feeding birds are crowded together near the shore. Arrive at low tide and see tiny specks of birds on the horizon—they follow the tide out, probing frantically at newly uncovered mud. Some two dozen species of shorebirds stop at Bowerman Basin: sandpipers, dunlin, dowitcher, whimbrel, semipalmated plover, phalarope, dabbling ducks, peregrines, eared grebe, Franklin's gull, and black-bellied plovers may all be seen. The majority of birds, brown-backed and white-bellied with rusty brown caps, are western sandpipers, seven species of which visit Grays Harbor. As many as a million individual birds stop here.

Although all the shorebirds look much alike to the untrained eye, their special adaptations are visible in the different shapes and lengths of their bills and their different feeding styles. Sandpipers tend to be methodical feeders; dunlins, with slightly longer bills, peck and dash, peck and dash; dowitchers, with even longer bills, probe in a quick up-and-down motion. Phala-ropes spin around in the water, stirring up food. Dunlins may stay for the entire winter, all fifty thousand of them. Peregrines hover around the area and stir up the population when they take a meal.

Just what are these birds eating? Mud flats are rich communities. Each square foot is packed with amphipods, clams, marine worms, and a variety of other small crustaceans and mollusks. The primary food here

Spotted sandpiper

is a small amphipod. We know why they are eating—it is another 1,500 miles to nesting sites in Alaska. They may stop to rest and feed briefly on the way north, but the fat packed on in a week or two at Bowerman Basin is their main source of energy for the grueling flight.

The Aberdeen sewage treatment ponds for industrial waste are another local site that often harbors unusual bird species. Both the stilt sandpiper and the Hudsonian godwit have been seen there.

6

KAPOWSIN FLOATING BOG

Community: Bog, freshwater marsh
Size: 513 acres
Ownership: State of Washington
Season: Available all year
Cautions: Accessible only by boat; stumps in the lake
Facilities: Picnic grounds, boat access
Fee: None
Hours: Always open
Maps: DeLorme Atlas and Gazetteer, page 47
Highlights: Floating bog, sundew, Labrador tea
Nearest Town: Kapowsin

Located on Lake Kapowsin, this bog is approximately 15 miles south of Puyallup off Meridian Avenue (Highway 161). Turn left off 161 onto the

Kapowsin Highway; after passing the blinking red light by the Kapowsin Tavern, continue northeast to the first turnoff to Lake Kapowsin. A road full of gargantuan potholes leads to a parking area with a boat launch.

A kayak or canoe is the best vehicle for exploring this bog, since one must slip into the cracks between huge old floating logs at the north end of the lake. After launching your boat, go left; paddling along the lake shore on a clear day provides a view of underwater stumps from the trees that previously grew here and which now release organic matter into the lake. Many of these now punctuate the water's surface and thus emphasize the need for measured movement.

The bog is penned behind a flotilla of giant logs, and openings to it remain hidden. Years of floating on the lake have brought these logs into an equilibrium with the water. During the summer they rise a little higher in the water, and during the rainy, humid winter they sink a little lower. Although not a classic bog, the logs have become a substitute for a depression on solid land and are overlaid with moss and acid-loving plants.

As you pole and shunt yourself through corridors of logs, watch for the carnivorous sundews. These improbable plants have slender hairs on their leaves that culminate in round, red, viscid drops. Resembling dew and magnifying any available light, these structures capture unwary insects as they wander over the plant, holding them fast until the elongated structure folds over and, after a period of time, dissolves them into the plant. Although the sundews use some nutrients from the trapped insects, these insects remain peripheral to the plant's survival—rather like the frosting on a cake.

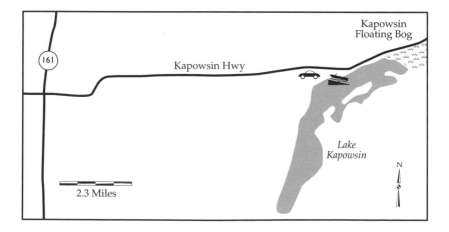

Kapowsin Floating Bog

Labrador tea also grows on these logs. Although this shrub can reach 3 feet in height, here it seldom surpasses a foot and a half. Elongated oval leaves, dark green and leathery, curve under along their margins. Pale, feltlike hairs mat the underside of the leaf. Early explorers concocted a hot brew from the leaves. Stunted red alder and round-leafed willows often grow alongside the Labrador tea, creating small screens between one log and another. Scattered about on logs and plant leaves are shells from the orb snail. Often reaching 2 inches in diameter, this snail is consumed by a variety of birds.

Along the edge of the bog you may hear a kingfisher calling. Trees hanging over the edge of the water provide a convenient perch from which it can dive for fish. The huge yellow water iris grows here, sometimes on solid ground, sometimes floating on a mass of rhizomes. The flower looks as if it is a domestic plant that has escaped the harness. Iris and masses of cattails line the sides of Lake Kapowsin and reveal its gradually sloping margins. The lake is a good place to watch ducks and Canada geese, and the aquatic plant population reflects the richness and warmth of the lake water.

The yellow water lily spreads its huge waxy leaves over the surface and provides a landing surface for dragonflies, beetles, and minute gnats that feed on plants. From among these oval, shield-shaped leaves, the water lily's bold yellow flowers rise just above the water's surface. Water lily stems are connected to the center of the leaf, much like those of a nasturtium, and the stems and leaf undersides are coated with a thick, clear jelly. Pondweeds possess two kinds of leaves: the waxy upper ones are oval and may float on the surface, but the lower leaves are linear and grasslike. Ducks love seeds from this plant and, by eating them, help distribute it to new freshwater habitats.

Beyond the endless corridors of the floating bog, other margins of the lake have many aquatic plants characteristic of shallow ponds and also exhibit the flying, swimming, and diving insects commonly found in marshy areas.

7

MCNARY NATIONAL WILDLIFE REFUGE

Community: Freshwater marsh
Size: 3,600 acres
Ownership: U.S. Department of the Interior, Fish and Wildlife
   Service
Season: Closed during nesting season
Cautions: No boats or campfires
Facilities: Parking
Fee: None
Hours: Daylight
Maps: Local
Highlights: Spring and fall bird migrations
Nearest Town: Pasco

From Pasco, go 2.5 miles southeast on Highway 12. Turn left on Maple Street, then left onto South Lake Road and right into the parking lot.

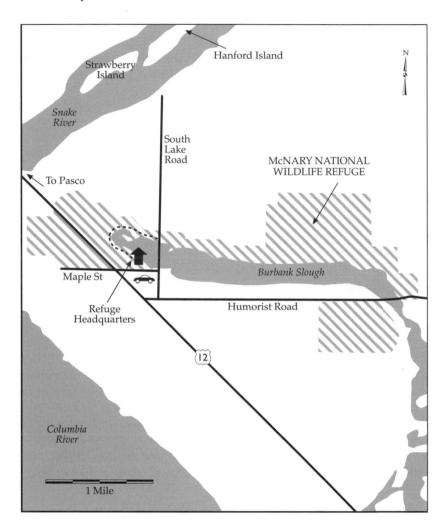

Cross the road to follow the mile-long Burbank Slough Interpretive Trail. The refuge headquarters is on the left, just before the corner of Maple Street and South Lake Road.

McNary Refuge is sited where the Snake River joins the Columbia and is clearly a former channel that has since been partially turned to land. The wildlife refuge consists of the 150-acre Burbank Slough and several thousand acres of surrounding agricultural fields in combination with the Strawberry Island and Hanford Island divisions.

McNary National Wildlfe Refuge

The trail starts out in a mown area separated from the water by massive stands of giant rush. Bird voices can be heard on the water side as various ducks make a living in the reeds. A large part of this refuge consists of agricultural uplands, which provide food and rest areas for migrating waterfowl. Habitat types are diverse and include open water, river islands, grassy uplands, and marshes.

Tall wheat grass, alfalfa, clover, and corn all provide shelter on adjacent acreage. Damage to local farm crops is reduced by raising food for migrating waterfowl on the refuge. Mowing shorelines and burning dead vegetation reduce unproductive areas and provide more feeding space for waterfowl. Glimpses of the open water are framed with cattails and 7-foot-tall *Phragmites* grass, when small openings are mowed out from the main path. Twenty-five species of waterfowl move through this area during migration, including gadwalls, shovelers, teals, pintails, mallards, ring-necked ducks, goldeneyes, redheads, canvasbacks, buffleheads, and lesser scaup. Tundra swans may be seen in October, and white pelicans sometimes spend the winter. Killdeer, American avocet, long-billed curlew, and burrowing owls also nest here.

Toward the western end of the slough, open fields give way to willows and Russian olive trees, providing additional cover for dove and quail. The far side of the slough opens up again with views of the water and the attending birds, the mile-long trail ending at South Lake Road. A short walk along the road ends at the parking lot.

8

MERCER SLOUGH
Bellefields Nature Park

Community: Forested swamp, freshwater marsh fringing the slough
Size: 50 acres
Ownership: City of Bellevue, managed by the Bellevue Parks
   Department
Season: Open all year
Cautions: None
Facilities: Trails, interpretive signs
Fee: None
Hours: Always open
Maps: Bellevue Parks
Highlights: Skunk cabbage, boardwalks, birds
Nearest Town: Bellevue

Leave I-405 at exit 12; turn west on Southeast 8th Street and then south onto 118th Avenue Southeast at the next intersection. Less than a mile down the road is a parking area on the right.

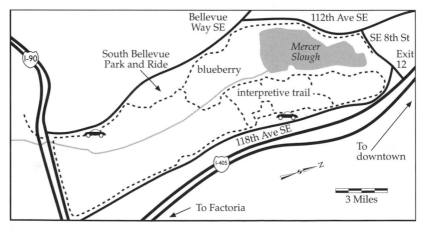

Great blue heron at Mercer Slough

A heavenly scent fills the air here, sometimes sweet, sometimes pungent, but always green and vibrantly alive. Sounds of the highway are ever present, and occasional views of hillsides packed with houses remind the walker of how lucky we are to have this small park.

Descend through a cool green forest of red cedars and bigleaf maples, both species disappearing abruptly at the base of the hill. Much of the park is a thicket of bitter cherry, ash, alder, red-osier dogwood, and bramble fruits. The luscious-looking fruits of the twinberry bush are everywhere. They are edible but not particularly tasty. Huge leaves of skunk cabbage line the paths, creating an almost tropical mood, and sturdy clumps of the bright green lady fern are scattered throughout.

A springy trail with boardwalks over the wettest bits circles the perimeter of the park for about 1 mile. Small loops and clearings maintained by the Parks Department allow additional explorations. As the trail nears the slough, put conversation on hold and approach the water's edge quietly. Ducks, coots, and geese are numerous in spring and fall. In early summer, ducklings and goslings paddle about in small flotillas. Herons pose motionlessly and watch for a long moment before stepping behind a screen of cattails, and muskrat swim through the middle of the slough. Hungry mosquitoes make long observation uncomfortable.

Be sure to take the bridge over the slough. It allows a good view up and down the slough and then leads to a wide, sturdy boardwalk that winds out into a huge hardhack thicket. Off to one side are blueberry fields, and everywhere in the distance is civilization. Yet in sight of all this a hawk perches on top of a snag and scans for mice, and birds flit through the bushes and over the boardwalk. Joggers make the loop trip in under 10 minutes, but set aside at least an hour to wander and appreciate this lovely wetland.

9

MUDDY MEADOWS TRAIL AND TAKH TAKH MEADOWS

Community type: Wet meadow
Size: 50 acres
Ownership: Gifford Pinchot National Forest, Goat Rocks
    Wilderness
Season: Late May to October
Cautions: Biting bugs, early mud, heavy horse use
Facilities: None; primitive campground with pit toilets (Spring
    Creek) less than 0.5 mile away
Fee: None
Hours: Always open
Map: Gifford Pinchot National Forest Service map
Highlights: Elk, hummingbirds, camas lilies, orchids, view
Nearest Town: Randle

From Randle, follow FR 23 for about 33 miles, and turn left on FR 2329 toward Takhlakh Lake and Midway Meadows. At about 6 miles, look for a sign on the left for Muddy Meadows Trail; the trailhead is a short mile down the road at a dead end. This quiet, short walk has access to

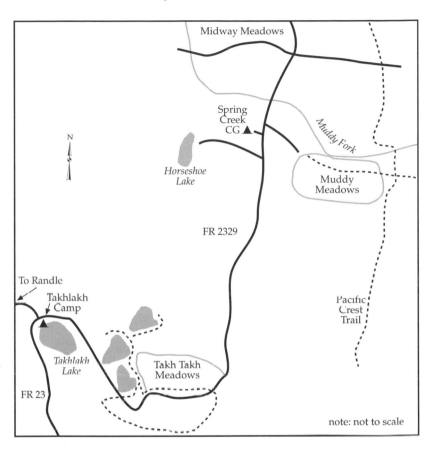

the Pacific Crest trail and a stunning view of Mount Adams. It's also close to Takhlakh Lake and other interesting wetlands: Chain of Lakes and Takh Takh Meadows. The meadow is at an elevation of 4,500 feet, and many lovely alpine and subalpine plants grow here.

This is a walk for the slow kind of day when the miles don't count. The trail begins at the edge of Muddy Meadows, and early in the season intensive horse traffic magnifies its muddy condition. Watch for elk tracks overlaying the horseshoe prints—an early-morning visit will reveal the elk browsing along the edges.

As your gaze sweeps over the meadow, the predominant impression is of rushes, but a closer look singles out a haze of blue. This is the camas lily; it grows from a bulb that was one of the staple foods of Native Americans. Easily identified by its vivid blue flowers when in bloom,

Mount Adams from Muddy Meadows

after the flowering stalks wither it is difficult to distinguish from death camas. Death camas has a stalk of creamy white flowers and contains poisonous alkaloids—do not eat this bulb.

As you walk along looking down, you will find many kinds of plants nestled among the sedges and grasses. Creeping white clover extends its coverage with running stems that drop roots at each joint. Field buttercup claims many acres of wet meadows by producing abundant runners and a set of roots each time a runner touches ground. Sometimes confused with buttercup, silverweed grows among stunted hardhack shrubs, and blue-flowered lupine stems poke up everywhere.

Large copper butterflies and a smaller cousin, the blue butterfly, drift and rest continuously, and the air buzzes with the sound of working bees. Tiny hungry mosquitoes and no-see-ums circle and settle each time you stop—now is the time for the insect repellent.

A thick mat of tiny moss-like leaves supports the minute yellow-orange flowers of bog St. John's wort. This tough little plant also grows in bogs, and under some conditions it can grow to 3 inches tall. Related to

Red-tailed hawk

Klamath weed, a plant that poisons livestock, bog St. John's wort has not been identified as poisonous.

Near the southern edge of the meadow is a stand of cottongrass, another member of the huge sedge family but with stems often not as markedly triangular. The "cotton" consists of bristles that surround the fruits. Also here is the first large stand of false hellebore, which looks similar to corn but is not a grass at all. By late July it will be 4 to 6 feet tall and will bear heads of small greenish flowers. Trimmed shapes illustrate this plant's attractiveness to deer and elk. Look for the pinkish-purple inside-out flower of the shooting star in low, bare areas.

On the east side of the trail, scattered like tiny light poles in a parking lot, are stems of penstemon. These plants, with their clusters of blue tubular flowers with pink throats, are members of the snapdragon family. Penstemons that grow on moist stream banks are often large and showy; this species is small but eye-catching.

At the very southern end of the meadow, just as the land rises slightly and the conifers start to take over, a willow thicket marks a small stream. Sparkling white bog orchids light up the meadow, and shooting stars erupt out of muddy circles. Lupines line the trail, each with leaves as large as your hand, each holding a glistening drop of water in the center. Bright red Indian paintbrush and purple asters draw hummingbirds to the meadow.

The smaller Takh Takh Meadows supports a similar array of plants. Go back south on FR 2329 for about 2 miles; if you reach the turnoff for Takhlakh Lake, you've gone too far. The trail begins on the right side of the road. The west fork of Adams Creek runs through the meadows, which are bounded on the west by strange, huge mounds of black rocks. A path wanders around the base of one rock pile through a narrow band of subalpine fir, pink heather, beargrass, and huckleberries. The meadow proper is dominated by sedges and rushes and an assortment of buttercup, veronica, shooting star, bog orchids, and hellebore.

10

Nisqually National Wildlife Refuge

Community: Salt marsh, forested swamp, wetland meadow
Size: 2,948 acres
Ownership: U.S. Department of the Interior, Fish and Wildlife Service
Season: Open all year, seasonal closure of the dike trail
Cautions: Winter flooding of river trail, no pets
Facilities: Interpretive literature and visuals
Fee: $2.00 per family
Hours: Daylight
Maps: Local
Highlights: Raptors, waterfowl, estuary
Nearest Town: Lacey

Traveling either direction on I-5, take the Nisqually Refuge exit (no. 114) and follow signs to the refuge parking lot. From the parking lot, take a short walk to the information kiosk to read about the salt marsh system. The Brown Farm was established here in 1902, and the salt marsh was diked to claim farming land. The refuge now includes the original farm, the freshwater forested swamp along the river, and the salt marsh along Puget Sound. It is sandwiched between the Nisqually River on the east and McAllister Creek on the west.

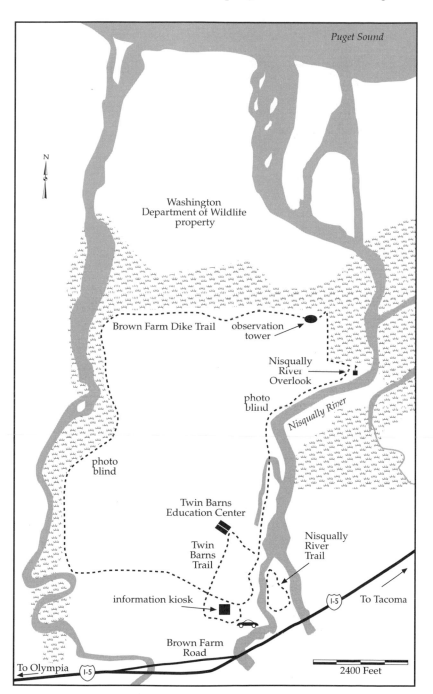

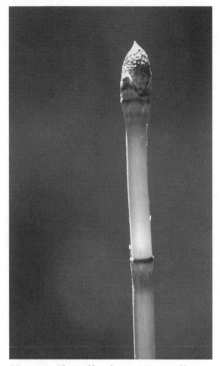

Horsetail stalk along Nisqually River Trail

A short trail through the remnants of the original Brown Farm orchard and along a cattail marsh brings one to the Nisqually River Trail. This 0.5-mile trail through a forested swamp is lined with the plants found along the flooded banks of a river. This is a riparian community. As late as August you may see the vivid orange flowers of the jewelweed, or touch-me-not. Its seed pods mature until the slightest touch explodes the pod, spraying seeds across the landscape.

Horsetail also grows along this trail. Tall, slender green stems rise up 4 feet from the ground, ridged and with tiny domes on top. No branches are visible. During the Carboniferous period (over 300 million years ago) its relatives were trees that grew 40 feet tall. Today's horsetails tend to follow the damp, spreading by underground rhizomes. Their high silica content made them attractive as scrubbers to early settlers. Very tolerant of heavy metals, they were also used to assay for gold.

There is solid evidence of the last cresting of the river—skunk cabbage leaves and other plants are coated with a film of dried river silt, and the black cottonwood tree trunks have high-water marks of grey mud. The trail along the banks of the Nisqually River passes nest boxes for wood ducks, nailed 8 to 10 feet up in the trees. Mosquitoes find this a propitious habitat, with its offerings of human blood passing through the woods.

Continue walking right after exiting the River Trail—the Twin Barns Education Center is located here and is open to visitors on weekends. Follow the Brown Farm Dike Trail (5.5 miles) on the top of the dike, first along the river through open meadows and borders of wild rose, maple and willow. At about 2 miles is an elevated observation tower. Look out toward Puget Sound behind a changing screen of apple, willow, and meadow grasses where the inlets and islands of the estuary are in evidence. Silt is deposited here, and tidal currents change the shape of the barely emergent soft ground. Most of the land caught in the braidings of the estuary is covered with glasswort intermixed with brass buttons. Both plants are succulent; both are short and grow in dense stands. They give these hummocks the appearance of tightly trimmed grass.

Although migrating waterfowl use the adjoining fields to feed and rest, many will be found swimming in these inlets and resting on the estuarine islands. Altogether 176 species of birds have been observed at Nisqually, with an additional thirty-six other species listed as accidental. All the Pacific Northwest salmon and trout are found here in the estuary nursery. The diked fields are alive with shrews, moles, eastern cottontails, snowshoe hares, many mammals including beaver, river otters, minks and muskrats, and an abundance of bats—six species, to be exact. The refuge seethes with life.

11

OZETTE LAKE
Ahlstrom's Prairie

Community: Bog, forested swamp
Size: 160 acres
Ownership: Olympic National Park
Season: Open all year
Cautions: Boardwalk extremely slippery; no bikes,
    dogs, or weapons
Facilities: Campground, ranger station, telephone, rest rooms
Fee: None
Hours: Always open
Maps: USGS Lake Ozette
Highlights: Swamp gentian, sundew, Labrador tea
Nearest Town: Ozette

From Clallam Bay take Highway 112 to Sekiu. About 1 mile west of Sekiu turn south on Hoko-Ozette Road. Drive 21 miles to the road's end, where there are a campground, a ranger station, and trail heads. A natural history exhibit at the ranger station describes the area and its wildlife. To find the boardwalk, follow trail signs for Cape Alava. This is a multipurpose hike for all seasons, with bog, forested swamp, and ocean beach

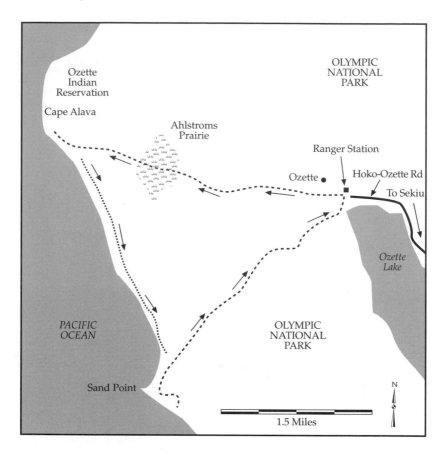

all found in just over 3 miles, or a loop hike of 9.5 miles can make a long day trip or an overnight. Overnight backcountry trips require a permit.

The boardwalk begins in wet coastal forest, with huge spruce and red cedar trees and a heavy undergrowth of salal and Olympic huckleberry. Lower areas are wet enough to be labeled forested swamp. Here are the huge leaves of skunk cabbage and clumps of sharp-edged sedges. The familiar lady fern is absent, but deer fern is abundant, and mosses and liverworts cover the forest floor and fallen logs and form bright carpets around edges of pools. The numerous creeks and pools on the way are a clear, peat-colored brown.

At 2 miles the boardwalk emerges into a broad, open bog-prairie. Lars Ahlstrom settled here in 1902 and remained until 1958. The prairie is partially ancient lake bed slowly being filled in and partially land cleared by Ahlstrom for pasture. Trees are invading the bog, predominantly spruce,

Boardwalk at Ozette Lake

hemlock, and cedar. Drier ridges support bracken fern and salal, but the lower areas are dominated by Labrador tea shrubs with an understory of sphagnum moss. Open areas of sphagnum are overlain with a tangle of cranberry, sedges, and rushes. Late in the summer, the meadow is brilliant with the blue of swamp gentian. Look for sundew, not terribly common in this old, dry bog but present, and for sticky asphodel, with its greenish white flowers or, in late summer, red berries. At the far edge of the bog are remnants of Ahlstrom's cabin and outbuildings.

The bog is less than 0.5 mile long. Once through it, the boardwalk enters trees again for the final mile and a bit to the ocean. There is plenty of exploring to do here and many camp sites too, except on a mid-summer weekend. Return by the same trail or trek the beach 3 miles south to Sand Point and then return to Ozette on 3 miles of boardwalk through wet forest.

12

PADILLA BAY NATIONAL ESTUARINE RESEARCH RESERVE

Community: Eelgrass beds, salt marsh
Size: 11,000 acres on bay, 200 upland acres
Ownership: Washington State Department of Ecology, administration by National Oceanic and Atmospheric Administration (NOAA) under U.S. Department of Commerce
Season: Open all year
Cautions: Seasonal hunting (October through January); no motorized vehicles or horses; leashed dogs
Facilities: Bayview State Park nearby, Breazeale Interpretive Center, benches, picnic tables, informative signs
Fee: None
Hours: Always open
Maps: Available at interpretive center
Highlights: Birds, harbor seals, estuarine plant and animal life
Nearest Town: Bayview

To get to Padilla Bay, take Highway 20 west from I-5 for about 6 miles, turn right on Bayview-Edison Road, and go north for about 4 miles. Visit the Breazeale Interpretive Center first; operating hours are 10:00 A.M. to 5:00 P.M. Wednesday through Sunday. The interpretive center has displays of the various animals you may see, saltwater aquaria, informative material, and a special hands-on children's room. Just across the street from the center is a wheelchair-accessible observation deck and a spiral staircase to the beach (open April through October). A short upland forest trail near the center has a trail guide corresponding to numbered sites along the trail.

Padilla Bay has a bit of something for everyone: rocky shores, mud flats, eelgrass beds, salt marshes, sloughs, farm fields and hedgerows, forests, birds, trails, and observation decks. A state campground within a mile of the interpretive center makes it easy to spend a day or two here and take in the full scope of the bay.

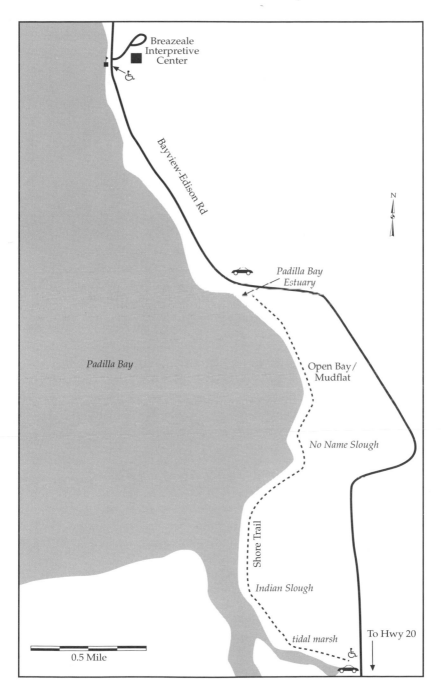

Breazeale
Interpretive
Center

Bayview-Edison Rd

N

Padilla Bay
Estuary

Padilla Bay

Open Bay /
Mudflat

No Name Slough

Shore Trail

Indian Slough

tidal marsh

To Hwy 20

0.5 Mile

To see the range of communities on Padilla Bay, take the 4.5-mile round-trip Shore Trail, which begins 1.1 miles south of the interpretive center off Bayview Edison Road. The trail is also accessible from the south end of the bay, where there is a gated handicapped parking lot near the intersection of Bayview-Edison Road and Highway 20. You will have to check out a key for the gate at the interpretive center. (**Note:** The gate is heavy and may not be readily moveable by a person in a wheelchair.) There are rest rooms at the center and porta-potties at both ends of the trail.

Grasshopper

A wide, white path on top of a dike, with interpretive signs and viewing benches, the Shore Trail scarcely requires a guide. To make this a wetland learning and appreciation experience, step off the path occasionally. Let the mud suck at your shoes as you look for shore crabs under the rocks. Feel the microscopic slime on the eelgrass blades and notice the thousands of mud snails littering the surface of the flat. At low tide, with miles of mud flats to feed on, most birds will be near the water's edge and appear to you as mere specks on the horizon. But near high tide, take a seat, apply binoculars to eyes, and watch the variety of birds feasting on the abundant food supply. Padilla Bay is an important stopover for migratory birds.

The eelgrass beds of Padilla Bay support thousands of brant in winter and spring as birds move up and down the Pacific flyway. Yellow-billed loons and canvasbacks are easily found along with huge flocks of dunlins, black-bellied plovers, and Eurasian wigeon. Along the roads and around Edison are prime sites for snowy owls, trumpeter swans, peregrines, and gyrfalcons. Samish Island hosts a great blue heron rookery, and the birds are often seen in the surrounding sloughs. Summer brings glaucous-winged gulls and Caspian terns.

At about 1.8 miles (counting from the north end), serious tidal salt marsh begins; there were bits and pieces earlier, perched on the tops of dredge spoil islands. Notice the zones of plants in this area: near the trail, blue-green, stiff beachgrass with its sharply pointed leaves and bold seed heads; a wide bank of pickleweed with scattered arrow-grass thrusting through it; then a final band of stiff, dusty green saltgrass in the area of highest salinity.

Padilla Bay, south end

13

POTHOLES RESERVOIR AND COLUMBIA NATIONAL WILDLIFE REFUGE

Community: Freshwater marsh
Size: Potholes—33,500 acres; Columbia—35,000 acres
Ownership: U.S. Bureau of Reclamation; maintained by
   Washington State Department of Fish and Wildlife
Season: All year
Cautions: Ticks, rattlesnakes
Facilities: Overnight camping, rest rooms, and showers at state park;
   latrines at lakes; Soda Lake overnight, no other campgrounds
Fee: Overnight fee at state park; none for the lakes
Hours: Always open
Maps: Available at headquarters
Highlights: Oasis for birds, mammals, humans
Nearest Town: Moses Lake

From Moses Lake go west on I-90 to the Dodson Road exit; turn left and
go approximately 10 miles to the intersection of Frenchman Hills Road.

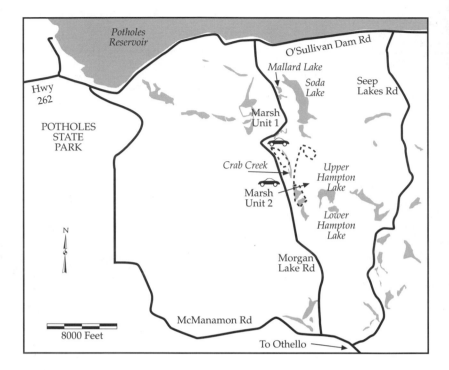

Turn left on Frenchman Hills Road, which turns into Highway 262. Continue east to Potholes State Park. To visit the Columbia National Wildlife Refuge, continue east on Highway 262 over O'Sullivan Dam. At the sign for Marsh Unit 1, turn right, and follow the road. The best map for this area is available from the Columbia National Wildlife Refuge headquarters in Othello.

Potholes State Park is best experienced by boat; this provides the opportunity to nose around the countless small coves and inlets of the reservoir. Sloping banks tend to be very muddy and soft but are interesting places to look for waterfowl. Several kinds of willow grow here, and the desert influence is seen in their very narrow leaves, which do not heat up as easily, and in the heavy covering of hairs on many of the leaves. These hairs reduce water loss from the leaves and give them a silvery, reflective appearance. Russian olive trees, an introduced species that thrives in eastern Washington, also has a silvery pelt. Hardy carp are much in evidence here. They are able to live in low oxygen levels and to tolerate extreme temperature variations, high levels of suspended silt, and water pollution. They eat all kinds of things: plant fragments, seeds, midges, caddis flies, clams, and assorted detritus. Several commercial fisheries in eastern Washington process carp into dry meal fish food.

Exploring Marsh Units 1 and 2 is an opportunity to compare the dry volcanic steppe plants with those found growing around and in the many small lakes. Each lake is a gem, brilliant in its contrasting greens and blues, made more vivid by the grays and browns surrounding it. The scenic drive past Soda and Mallard Lakes on the left continues down Morgan Lake Road past Scabrock Lake to a parking lot. This is the start of a short loop trail of less than a mile. Farther on, at the next parking lot, another double loop trail goes north nearly to Migraine Lake and down around the Hampton lakes and along Crab Creek. Many insects live along these lake margins, feeding on other insects hatched in the warm shallow water. This is good bird-watching territory—you are sure

Pothole framed by columnar basalt

to see the black-crowned night heron and the great blue heron hunting. The pied-billed grebe nests in the area; other grebes are uncommon. Badger have been sighted, and long-tailed weasels are common.

Continue down Morgan Lake Road to its intersection with McManamon Road. To continue the scenic drive turn right; to reach Othello, turn left. To visit many more lakes and ponds, turn left on Seep Lakes Road, which eventually rejoins O'Sullivan Dam Road (Highway 262).

14

QUINAULT LAKE LOOP TRAIL

Community: Forested swamp
Size: 12 acres
Ownership: U.S. Department of Agriculture, Forest Service, Quinault Ranger District
Season: Open all year
Cautions: None, mostly level trail
Facilities: Campground, ranger station, store, lodge
Fee: None
Hours: Always open
Maps: Local
Highlights: Cedar snags, skunk cabbage, giant trees surrounding wetland
Nearest Town: Quinault

From Hoquiam drive approximately 30 miles north on Highway 101, turn right onto South Shore Road, and follow the signs to Quinault Lake Lodge. The trail starts across the street from the lodge.

In one sense, the entire Quinault Valley could be considered a wetland—the average annual rainfall is 140 inches. Even in the relatively dry summer months, frequent fogs condense on the trees and drip to the forest floor. The Quinault Lake Loop Trail leads through a section of the temperate rain forest for which the Olympic Peninsula is so famous. The trail has several loops and can be as short as 3.5 miles, or as long as 7 miles if the side trails and loops are taken.

For a little over a mile, stroll through typical temperate rain forest vegetation—huge western red cedar, Douglas-fir, Sitka spruce, and hemlock trees, all heavily draped with mosses and lichens. The single largest known specimen of each of these four types of trees exists in this moist strip of land along the Pacific Coast. The understory is composed

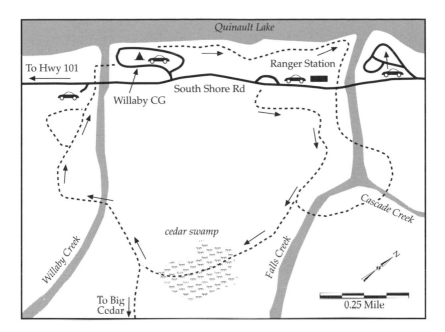

of salmonberry, devil's club, sword fern, deer fern, oxalis (shamrock), and many moss species.

Moving quickly across the trail as they go about their business are shiny black ground beetles, about half an inch long. They are predators that eat mostly other insects but sometimes dine on a slug. They consume some of our worst pests, including cutworms and gypsy moth larvae.

The numerous rotting fallen trees seen at almost every step along the trail support dense growths of tree seedlings and are known as nurse logs. Most of the seedlings are hemlocks, which are highly tolerant of shade. Unlike Douglas-fir, hemlock seedlings grow happily in the shade.

Follow the trail to the right to the cedar swamp boardwalk. The log just to the left at the end of the first boardwalk section has the usual array of mosses and tree seedlings and some unusual flat, light green, leafy plants with a leathery appearance, called liverworts. They are related to the mosses, and they grow prolifically in moist environments.

The next two sections of boardwalk are in the heart of the cedar swamp. The largest and most dramatic herbaceous plant is skunk cabbage. It flowers very early in the spring, with an unusual bright yellow bract surrounding the greenish spikelike flower stalk. The huge green leaves persist into September. Wetland delineators love to see skunk

Deer fern surrounded by oxalis

cabbage: its presence indicates the strong likelihood that the area is a wetland.

The tall, silvery dead trees are red cedar snags. Cedar grows reasonably well even when stagnant water occurs at the surface during the winter months, but year-round exposure to deeper water does kill the trees.

About 0.5 mile after the cedar swamp is an excellent example of a nurse log. Part of the log has been cut away to show the relationship between the "nursery" and the young tree growing on top. Eventually the fallen log will have rotted away entirely, leaving a row of trees on stilts.

The trail continues high above Willaby Creek gorge. The steep, moss-covered rock slopes teem with small hemlock trees, vine maples, and sword ferns, all clinging precariously to the wet walls. The next quarter-mile of trail crosses through several mini-swamps with salmon-berry canes, devil's club, and skunk cabbage in the understory.

At the end of Willaby Creek Gorge the trail intersects with South Shore Road. Maidenhair ferns grow at the base of the gorge walls. The trail goes under the road, passes through Willaby campground, and follows the shore of Quinault Lake for about 1 mile past willows, salmon-berry, and alder trees.

15

RIDGEFIELD WILDLIFE REFUGE, RIVER "S" UNIT

Community: Freshwater marsh, wet meadows
Size: 4,627 acres
Ownership: U.S. Department of the Interior, Fish and Wildlife Service
Season: Open all year, with seasonal closures during hunting season (by permit) and some areas closed from October 1 to April 15 to protect winter waterfowl
Cautions: No camping, no fires, no off-road driving, no artifact collecting, leashed pets only, restricted bicycling and horseback riding
Facilities: Information kiosk, parking, toilets, observation blinds, wheelchair-accessible blind, waterfowl hunting, fishing
Fee: None
Hours: Dawn to dusk
Maps: Available at the refuge office at 301 North 3rd Street in Ridgefield
Highlights: A variety of freshwater wetlands, extensive numbers of wintering waterfowl, migratory birds
Nearest Town: Ridgefield

From Seattle, take I-5 south to exit 14 (south of Woodland). Follow Highway 501 for 3 miles to Ridgefield. Turn left on South 9th Street and watch for the refuge sign on the right, about a mile down 9th. A kiosk at the first parking lot provides a map and information on some of the many

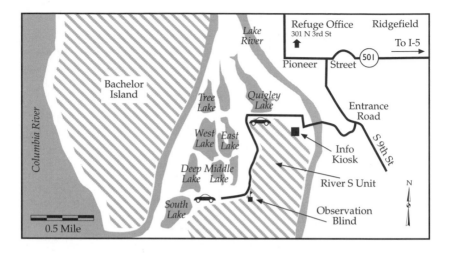

birds and other animals that use the refuge. About 2 miles of gravel road are open to visitor access.

River "S" and neighboring Bachelor Island are agriculturally managed portions of the refuge. They are diked to protect them from seasonal flooding by the Columbia River, and water levels in lakes and ponds are controlled by pumps. Crops are planted to provide optimal browse for waterfowl. There are no formal trails at the River "S" Unit, but footpaths run everywhere through the wet pastures and along the dikes. For a preliminary survey, drive to the end of the road and park in lot D.

Follow a farm track through a gate and circle left, along a slough. To the right is an extensive wet meadow thickly dotted with rushes and dipping down to a drainage area frequented by great blue herons. Follow the track for about 0.25 mile until it meets a fence; then turn right across the meadow and up onto the west dike. From here a trail runs through the woods to a beach along Lake River or continues out to the Columbia River. Bachelor Island, visible from this trail, is accessible by boat only, and visitors to the island must have a permit. Follow the dike back to a wide path running between shallow ponds, leading directly back to the parking lot.

The major attraction at the refuge is birds: migratory birds in spring and fall, nesting birds in summer, and overwintering birds. About 400 pairs of herons nest on Bachelor Island, and although their nests are hidden by the foliage of the cottonwood trees, the birds can be seen wading through shallow marshes year-round. Some twenty thousand ducks and thousands of the dusky subspecies of Canada goose winter at the refuge, along with thousands of tundra swans. Solitary sandpipers can also be found during migrations, along with white-fronted and snow geese. More sandhill cranes can be seen here than at any other location in Washington. Between early October and March, the 3-foot-tall bird with a red cap on its forehead feeds in the surrounding countryside and on the grain provided at the refuge. When flying, it stretches out its neck and legs, unlike the great blue heron.

Early morning and evening are the best times to watch for other animals, as well as being the optimal bird-watching hours. Mammals at the refuge include black-tailed deer, coyote, fox, raccoon, skunk, beaver (look for gnawed trees along the west dike), otter, and the nonnative nutria. Nutria are large aquatic rodents introduced from South America that live in burrows on the sides of dikes and ditch banks; their burrowing activities can cause considerable damage. Around dusk watch for bats out hunting for insects.

Ridgefield marshes

16

SCHRIEBERS MEADOW, MOUNT BAKER

Community Type: Wet meadow
Size: 400 acres
Ownership: Mount Baker Wilderness, within Mount Baker–
  Snoqualmie National Forest
Season: July through October
Cautions: Abrupt changes in weather, rugged landscape
Facilities: Latrines at trailhead parking lot
Fee: None
Hours: Always open
Maps: Hamilton Green Trails and Baker Pass USGS
Highlights: Views, berries, cottongrass
Nearest Town: Sedro Woolley

From Sedro Woolley travel east on Highway 20 for 15 miles and turn left
on Baker Lake Road. In 13 miles cross a cement bridge and enter the
Mount Baker–Snoqualmie National Forest. Turn left onto FR 12, travel
3 miles, and turn right onto FR 13. Follow the road to the end, about
5 miles.

The trail begins west of the road, crossing Sulphur Creek and ascend-
ing for a gentle 0.5 mile through trees, heather, and blueberries. Just as

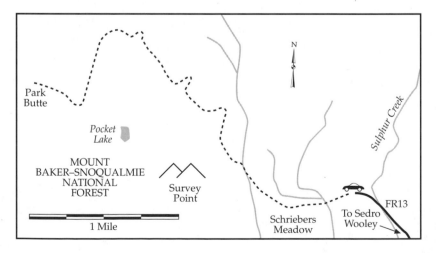

Adult crane fly
and larvae

the way opens up into the meadow proper, tiny ponds and seasonal ponds (marked by circular stands of grasses, sedges, or cottongrasses) begin to appear. At an elevation of 3,480 feet, this meadow shares many characteristics with other areas near Mount Baker. The weather station at Heather Meadows, at 4,150 feet, has recorded an average of 110 inches of precipitation and 116 inches of snowfall. Trees in this area include mountain hemlock, subalpine fir, and the occasional Alaska-cedar. Islands of trees are surrounded by stands of heather, blueberry, fescue, and black alpine sedge and dotted with monkeyflower, valerian, lupine, coltsfoot, and fireweed. Stunted willows and subalpine spirea occur. Wide swaths of marsh marigolds with big rounded leaves follow the slight contours around wet depressions. Stands of hellebore are thick, and elephant's head louseworts are thinly scattered between them. By early August many plants are already setting seed; it's a short growing season at this elevation.

The trail winds through the northern edge of the meadow for about 0.5 mile before entering forest again. The terrain here is fragile, so stay on established walkways. Paths take off to tiny ponds at frequent intervals, each one different enough to make a detour worthwhile. One pond has tiny lily pads; another is surrounded by the white, waving heads of cottongrass, suggesting the high soil acidity of a bog.

Hoary marmots are commonly seen, along with white-tailed ptarmigan, horned larks, American pipits, and rosy finch. Watch for dippers in Sulphur Creek, and spotted owls might be heard rather than seen. Golden eagles might fly by, and they, along with other raptors, are often announced by the whistling signals of the marmots. Evidence of pikas is seen in the small piles of grasses and sedges drying on piles of rocks, ready to be stored in burrows for the coming winter.

If you are in adequate physical condition, continue on to Park Butte Lookout, elevation 5,450 feet, and see the glaciers on Mount Baker, or just enjoy the surrounding rugged countryside.

Schriebers Meadow

17

SCRIBER LAKE CITY PARK

Community: Forested swamp, freshwater marsh
Size: 18 acres
Ownership: City of Lynnwood
Season: Open year-round
Facilities: Rest rooms, benches, sawdust walkways, docks
Fee: Free
Hours: 8:00 A.M. to dusk
Maps: Local
Highlights: Sculptures, observation dock
Nearest Town: Lynnwood

Right in the city of Lynnwood is a little gem of a park, built around a small lake and the creek that drains it. As an accompaniment to the natural wonders, the park service has installed a number of delightful iron benches and tables, all with wetland themes.

To reach Scriber Lake Park, leave I-5 North at exit no. 181, turn left on 44th Avenue towards Edmonds Community College, and then turn left (west) onto 196th Street. Follow 196th for 1.5 miles, turn left onto

Scriber Lake Road, also called 58th Avenue, turn left again on 198th, and go about two blocks to the park entrance.

The 1.2-mile loop walk begins in a lovely moist forest, dominated by alder trees with scattered Douglas-fir and hemlock. The trail dips downward, and shrubs that enjoy wet feet start appearing with great frequency: red elderberry, hardhack, and the most common shrub in the park, red-osier dogwood. The swamp looks lovely in the fall, with the thickets of bright red stems glowing around the silver-gray alder trunks.

A short trail to the left leads to an observation platform along the lake. The edge of the lake is choked with willows, cattails, and hardhack, and right at your feet are yellow iris. Bullfrogs rumble, and the melodic calls of cedar waxwings mix with cheery red-winged blackbird conversations.

Mixed throughout the forest are mountain ash trees, so common that we often think them to be native, but they are not. Cedar waxwings love the orange berries and feast on them, often to the point of intoxication. The overripe berries ferment in the birds' crop.

Look for blue darners and damselflies as they flit from branch to branch and patrol their areas. Scriber Creek is very sluggish here, wide and swampy, with overhanging willows and great clots of slimy algae and diatoms trailing from underwater sticks and stems. The creek joins Swamp Creek and eventually runs into the north end of Lake Washington. Spawning salmon were once seen regularly; now only the occasional fish makes its way here.

The trail advances into a boggy area, with waist-high sedges, enormous skunk cabbages, and the bright green of lady fern everywhere. A short observation trail to the right leads to a view of the North Lagoon, which was formed when 196th Street was built in the mid-1960s. The water is a murky brown from suspended peat particles, but peat moss

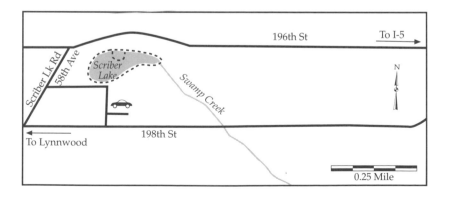

is not particularly plentiful here, and the unusual and beautiful plant species that often accompany it (sundew and Labrador tea) are missing.

Possibly the high point of the walk is the loop dock that leads out through the marsh into Scriber Lake. Yellow water lilies crowd close to the shore under overhanging willows. Dense stands of cattails extend along the entire lake edge, creating inviting perches for red-winged blackbirds. Mallard ducks clamor for bread, but other duck species are sometimes present. These include the colorful wood duck and the hooded merganser. Early in the morning you may see a muskrat sliding through the water, its snout creating a silent chevron ahead of it. Young salamanders idle in the shallows, and tiny fish dart frantically as a shadow passes overhead.

The trail passes next through a dense hardhack thicket, with the occasional wild rose peeking out. This is the drier end of the marsh; in another hundred years or so, it may be a young alder-hemlock forest.

The people of Lynnwood are proud of this park and very aware of the importance of the wetland. A number of interpretive signs along the trail provide information about the history of the area. There are plans to expand or improve the park, although with its wide, level sawdust paths and boardwalks it is difficult to see what else needs to be done to create an enjoyable and educational wetland site.

18

SINLAHEKIN WILDLIFE RECREATION AREA

Community: Freshwater marsh
Size: 14,000 acres
Ownership: Washington State Department of Fish and Wildlife
Season: Open all year
Cautions: Rough road, hunting in season
Facilities: Latrines at every lake, numerous primitive campsites
Fee: None
Hours: Always open
Map: Okanogan National Forest
Highlights: Birds, upland game: deer, bighorn sheep, bear
Nearest Town: Okanogan

From Okanogan take Highway 215 north and turn left onto Conconully Road on the west side of town. Follow this road to the community of

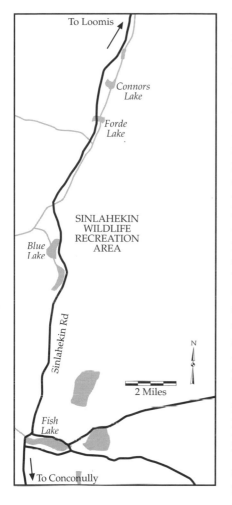

Conconully (approximately 20 miles), then turn north on Sinlahekin Road, a rough washboard that continues north through the wildlife recreation area to Loomis. The largest lakes, including Blue Lake, 9 miles south of Loomis, are on the west side of the road. There is an almost continuous string of marshes and small ponds on the east side. Not a day trip for most people, but worth a weekend drive and camp-out for the hardy, the Sinlahekin Wildlife Area is a long corridor along the Sinlahekin Creek, which lies in the Sinlahekin Valley. There are many acres of wetlands in this area of the Okanogan, most notably along the Okanogan River between Oroville and Ellisforde and along the Similkameen River north of Palmer Lake.

Birds to watch for in this area include grasshopper sparrows, horned larks, and long-billed curlews. Ruby-crowned kinglets and Lincoln's sparrows can also be seen. Not far from here in the Tiffany Mountain area is prime habitat for the diminishing lynx population in this state. Their habitat is being destroyed by logging. Gray catbird can be found in lakeside growth. Both yellow-headed blackbirds and red-winged blackbirds live and quarrel here.

Hard-stemmed bulrush is a giant among bulrushes. Growing up to 9 feet tall, it dominates the landscape and intrigues with its tall, cylindric stems that withstand wind and rain. Eastern Washington brings out the best in this bulrush; vast stands of it lace the margins of lakes and marshes. Because of the pithy nature of the stems, it has insulating

Cattail in bloom; male flower above female

qualities, and native people made extensive use of this plant for walls, roofs, mats, and door covers.

Cattails are another dominant plant in this landscape. Also known as reedmace, cattails have separated the sexes of their flowers. Male flowers are on the upper part of the spike and disintegrate, leaving the tip of the stem bare. The club-shaped female spike is our familiar brown cattail—the flowers turn into very tiny nutlets surrounded by hairs that allow them to float in wind or water. This plant provided native people with many functional items, from mats to blankets, and is our most familiar marsh plant.

19

SKAGIT WILDLIFE AREA

Community: Eelgrass beds, salt marshes, freshwater marshes,
    forested swamps
Size: 10,000 to 12,000 acres
Ownership: Washington State Department of Fish and Wildlife
Cautions: Hunting (deer, upland game birds, and waterfowl); no
    camping, no fires
Facilities: Latrine
Fee: None
Hours: Daylight hours only
Maps: Available at the office
Highlights: Variety of wetlands and cropland attracts many species
    of birds
Nearest Town: Conway

About 5 miles south of Mount Vernon exit I-5 at Conway and go west
on Fir Island Road. Turn left on Mann Road, which follows the edge of
Deepwater Slough and in about 2 miles arrives at a public hunting sign
at the wildlife area. Park here.

For a general exposure to what the Skagit Wildlife Area has to offer,
take the 2-mile loop walk. It starts near the office and follows Wiley
Slough, which is an extension of the west branch of the South Fork Skagit
River. The formerly rushing river is now spreading across flat delta land
as it moves quietly to the sea. The trail, really a narrow dirt road, swings
away from the river, but there is plenty of water near as numerous
sloughs and branches make their way seaward. Wetlands are on the
right, corn fields on the left, courtesy of extensive diking and agricultural management.

At 0.75 mile comes a three-way fork. The road to the right follows
the edge of Skagit Bay. Look over acres and acres of cattails as they grade
out into salt marsh and then to eelgrass flats. Here is a good area to watch
for brant and snow geese in the winter months.

The middle fork leads to the river's end, where fresh water meets
salt, another good snow goose spot. Shorebirding can also be good here
during spring and fall migrations. Time your walk for an incoming tide;
the flats here go forever, and at low tide, feeding birds are well beyond
visual range.

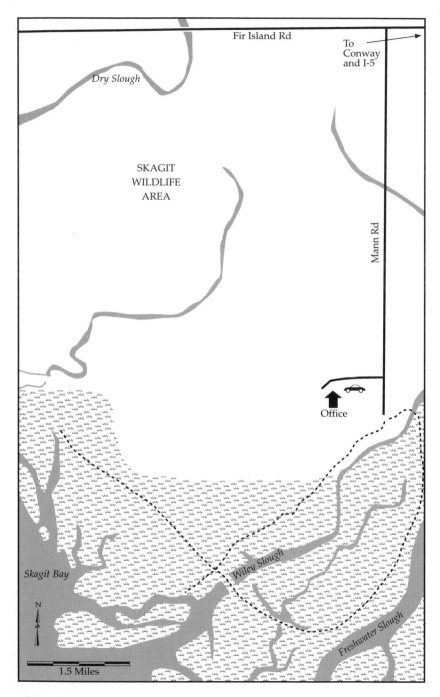

The left fork continues the loop trail. For 1.25 miles, you will pass through a superb mixture of freshwater marshes lining the sloughs and an increasingly brushy swamp composed of red-osier dogwood, willow, and alder. Look for sweetgale, the shiny-leafed bush just a few steps out of reach, and lots of rushes. Sporadic views and bridges lead to corn fields to the left; to the right is wet, wet, wet.

Common nesting birds of the area are robins, red-tailed hawks, spotted sandpipers, marsh wrens, and a variety of waterfowl, including mallards, blue-winged and cinnamon teal, and wood ducks. Bald eagles arrive in November to feed on spawning salmon. Float trips along the river to view the eagles are common in this area.

Short-eared owls and marsh hawks are quite common during the winter months. Snowy owls are seen here in flight years (those years when arctic lemming populations fall to low numbers). Use caution, but

Freshwater section of Skagit Wildlife Area

do come during the hunting season and winter months to see the impressive flocks of snow geese, interspersed with a few whistling swans.

20

SUMMIT LAKE
Mount Constitution, Orcas Island

Community: Bog
Size: 20 acres
Ownership: Washington State Parks Department
Season: Open all year
Cautions: Boggy areas along margin
Facilities: None
Fee: None
Hours: Always open
Maps: USGS
Highlights: Floating bog, salamanders, huge green algae
Nearest Town: Olga

From Anacortes, take the ferry to Orcas Island. Follow the Orcas-to-Olga Road, also known as the Horseshoe Highway, until you reach the intersection marked Mount Constitution; turn left. Summit Lake is three-quarters of the way to the top, at about 1,000 feet elevation, to the right of the road. Park along the edge and walk down to the lake on a gated-off road at the north end of the lake.

The north end of the lake has shallows punctuated with huge old semiburied logs providing easy pathways out onto the lake. Mare's tail rises from the bottom of the pond, creating a symmetrical forest of this graceful, narrow plant with whorled leaves. Some yellow pond lily and ovals of pondweed float on the lake surface around the end.

If you look down into the warm, shallow water you will see rough-skinned newts hanging motionless, while some sit out of water, sunning themselves on the logs, and others hold onto the vegetation, remaining still. When you move, they all dart away, but they soon settle down again. They are everywhere; the lake is full of newts! About 6 inches long, they have a rich chocolate color on the top of their body, with vivid orange along the sides and belly. When frightened, they dive and hide in the mud and in a curious plant growing all over the bottom of the lake.

This bright green plant consists of whorls of branches around a central stem and may grow to a foot tall. Touch it to feel its rough texture. This

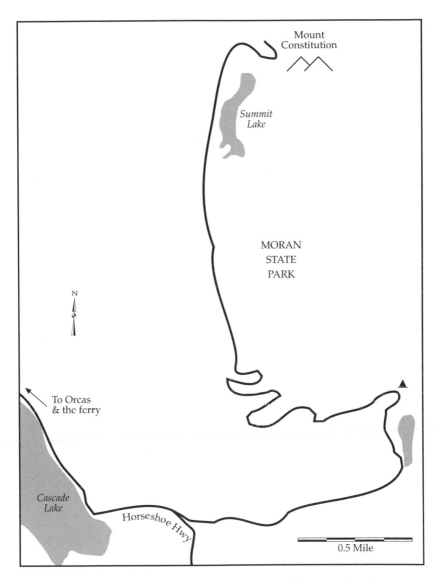

is a stonewort, *Chara*, a huge green alga that could be mistaken for a seed plant until one sees that it has no roots. *Chara* grows in water rich in calcium carbonate, and the rough texture is due to the deposition of lime in the plant's cells. The lime makes the plant unattractive to most plant eaters, but minute algae living on top of the *Chara* branches are eaten by a tiny crawling water beetle.

A corner of Summit Lake bog

The water beetle is a poor swimmer and is forced to return to the water's surface periodically to replenish the air carried below its wing covers and on the last segments of its hind legs. If it has adequate air on its body, it can use that to float to the surface, but it is otherwise forced to find a plant that extends to the surface and crawl up it for more oxygen. Because this brownish beetle is only 5 millimeters long, it is easily missed.

There is no trail entirely around the lake, but there is little underbrush, and the low light levels have killed most of the lower branches on the evergreens, making the forest floor fairly open. Follow the lake along the right and you will come to an area that juts out into the water. Some spots here have sphagnum moss growing along the shore—it is easily identified by its large, bold shape.

Out in the center of the lake is an island, really a floating bog, complete with stunted evergreens, bog Labrador tea, and a mass of cotton-grass plants, their heads of whitish bristles covering the landscape. The substrate in which they grow is made up of sphagnum moss, layers and layers of it, much of it dead but still supporting those plants growing on top.

This is a unique and fascinating lake that qualifies as a bog. The only other true bog left in the islands is in Beverton Valley on San Juan Island.

21
TENNANT LAKE NATURAL HISTORY INTERPRETIVE CENTER

Community: Freshwater marsh, forested swamp
Size: 200 acres
Ownership: Whatcom County Parks and Recreation Department
Season: Open all year
Cautions: No firearms; pets must be leashed
Facilities: Rest rooms, interpretive center, boardwalk
Fee: None
Hours: 8:00 A.M. to 9:00 P.M.; interpretive center noon to 5:00 P.M.
   Thursday through Sunday
Maps: USGS
Highlights: Boardwalk, Fragrance Garden
Nearest Town: Ferndale

From Bellingham, take I-5 north to exit 262 and head west on Main Street. Turn left on Hovander (under the railroad bridge) and then right on

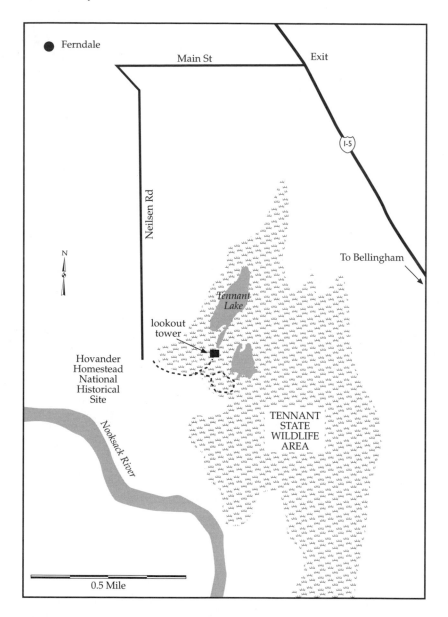

Neilsen Road. Tennant Lake is less than a mile from this intersection. Adjacent to the interpretive center is Hovander Homestead Park, a national historic site that features a restored house and barn, gardens, orchard, trails, fishing and picnic sites, and a play area. The two facilities easily merit an afternoon.

Before beginning the wetland walk, enjoy the unique Fragrance Garden in front of restored Neilsen House, which serves as the interpretive center. The Fragrance Garden was especially designed for the visually impaired, featuring plants with a variety of textures and fragrances. From the garden, a 0.5-mile trail and boardwalk circulates through a swamp and along the edges of a marsh. Tennant Lake itself is fairly distant and quite undisturbed, with Mount Baker presiding over all.

The walk first passes through a tall, waving stand of cattails mixed with reedgrass. A bridge crosses over a narrow waterway choked with duckweed, knotweed, and water lilies. Startled bullfrogs submerge with a shriek, and birds rustle busily in the grass. The tiny duckweed floating in otherwise clear patches of water is one of the tiniest flowering plants in the world; only two are smaller. One seldom sees the flowers; instead, it generally reproduces vegetatively. Up close it looks like large

Trailhead at Tenant Lake

green yeast budding off each other, with a tiny hairlike root hanging down from the center of the leaf underside.

The trail branches; a short walk to the left branch leads to an observation platform that looks across acres of water lilies toward the lake. The right boardwalk makes a long zig-zagging loop through the swamp. Initially

Bullfrog

under willow, alder, and wild cherry, the way soon opens out into a shrubby swamp dominated by aromatic sweetgale bushes. Mixed in is hardhack and a thick lower layer of silverweed and mare's tail. Between the shrubs are intervals of water lilies and occasional swaths of cattails. Snags everywhere support birdhouses. Swallows swoop continuously, red-winged blackbirds and wrens flit among the underbrush, bees buzz by, and butterflies touch down here and there. Tiny fish school around water lily stems, and the whole area is intensely alive and busy. It is easy, here, to understand the drive for wetland protection and conservation.

22

THELER WETLANDS
Belfair

Community: Salt marsh
Size: 50 acres
Ownership: Mason County
Season: Open year-round
Cautions: None
Facilities: Environmental classroom and exhibit area; latrines
Fee: None
Hours: Daylight
Maps: Local
Highlight: Boardwalk out over the marsh
Nearest Town: Belfair

From Bremerton, take Highway 3 to Belfair and park in the Theler Center lot on the right side of the road. A short gravel walk leads past the picnic area and playfield to the outdoor classroom. The trails, which provide wheelchair access, take visitors into a salt marsh formed at the confluence of the Union River and Hood Canal. The entire trail system loop is 4 miles long and consists of crushed rock and boardwalk.

From the outdoor classroom, a short loop takes you through a cedar and alder swamp and back to the beginning of the meadow. Take the South Tidal Marsh Trail to the left. It wanders through alder woods and passes extensive growth of water-hemlock. This is an extremely poisonous plant; do not handle or consume it. In spite of its potential impact, it is a lovely, airy member of the parsley family, crowned with delicate white flowers. Growing throughout this area are unusually huge willows, many of them several feet in circumference.

As the boardwalk moves out of the woods, the vegetation changes. Grasses give way to sedges and salt-tolerant grass as the observation deck terminates well out into the salt marsh. The effects of salt water inundation are marked by both the kinds of plants in the area and the indicators of invertebrate lives. Crab shells are tangled in the sedges; tracks are left in the soft, fine mud from wandering snails; and sea birds stand and watch. This deck provides a good observation point, allowing you to see the curve of the beach and the entry area of the Union River, far to the right. Return back down the trail and turn left to the Freshwater Marsh Trail.

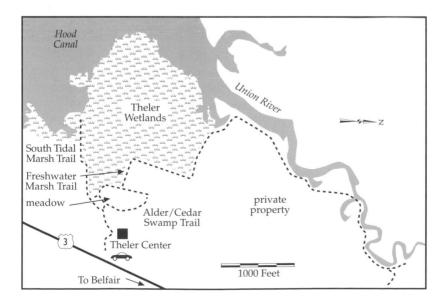

Tidal interchange at Theler Wetlands

The sweep of the salt marsh is laid out ahead as the trail leaves the woods and breaks through into the marsh. The trail follows the top of the levee. To the left is salt marsh, periodically inundated with salt water and tufted with sedges. As the levee angles out into the estuary, the character of the freshwater side of the marsh becomes more distinct.

Stands of the huge sedge called tule follow the edge of the trail. This is our tallest sedge, here growing to 6 feet. Also called hard-stemmed bulrush, tule was collected by native peoples for a variety of uses—walls, roofs, floor mats, and seat covers.

A sharp turn in the trail passes through a stand of crab apple, suckered from a few original trees. They show the power of the wind in their sculptured appearance. Short trails lead down from the levee into the salt marsh, where it is easy to get stuck in the finely sifted tidal mud.

At about 0.75 mile out, the Union River bank is reached. To the left the channel brings fresh water into contact with salt, and gradations of salt-tolerant plants are scattered throughout the immediate area. The trail turns right and follows the banks of the river. Studies done on this river water have shown unusual levels of heavy metals from an unknown source. Continuing along the trail, watch for ducks and great blue heron fishing in the shallows. The trail ends 2 miles from the origin. There is presently no loop, so retrace your steps and watch for raccoons to match the footprints in the mud. A pleasant walk, this wetland gives a fine sense of the openness, the smells, and the sounds of a salt marsh.

23

TURNBULL NATIONAL WILDLIFE REFUGE

Community: Freshwater marshes
Size: Approximately 15,500 acres, 2,200 acres open for public use
Ownership: U.S. Department of the Interior, Fish and Wildlife
    Service
Season: Open all year
Cautions: Ticks; no hunting, no fishing, no camping, no fires, no
    picnicking, no litter containers; leashed pets only
Facilities: Rest rooms (wheelchair-accessible), auto tour, boardwalk,
    trails, workshops and environmental education programs
Fee: $2.00 per vehicle between March 1 and October 31
Hours: Daylight hours only; gate opens at 5:30 A.M., closes
    at 10:00 P.M.
Maps: Available at the refuge gate and at headquarters
Highlights: Birds—migratory fowl, especially diving ducks; deer
    and elk; numerous ponds, marshes, and lakes
Nearest Town: Cheney

From Spokane take I-90 west, then turn on Highway 904 to Cheney. On the south edge of town, turn left on Cheney Plaza Road (there is a refuge sign) and drive 5.5 miles to the refuge entrance.

Turnbull National Wildlife Refuge was established in 1937 on land that had once been drained by pioneering farmers. They had expected the lake beds to produce rich crops but were quickly disappointed. Conservationists and sportsmen lobbied vigorously for the area to be returned to its natural state to provide food and habitat for year-round wildlife and migratory birds. Through their persistent efforts, the land is currently much as it was prior to white settlement.

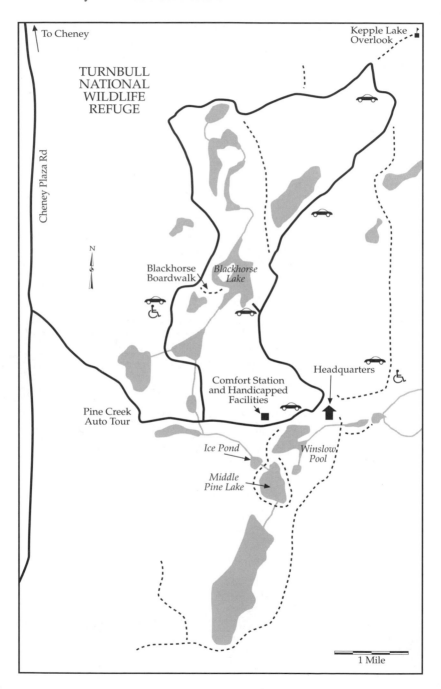

The Pine Creek Auto Tour is more than an excellent introduction to the refuge; it puts the visitor in touch with a large part of the refuge that is open to the public. Although it is only 5 miles long, allow at least an hour, as there are a number of places to stop and take short walks.

The drive begins in ponderosa pine, aspen, and roses mixed with grasses and wild geraniums. The air in mid-June is fragrant with rose and other sweet, subtly dry aromas. In 0.6 mile is a short turnoff to Blackhorse Lake. Standing tall around the lake are the round olive green stems of hardstem bulrush and the broad, brighter green leaves of cattails. These two species seem almost invariable in eastern freshwater wetlands. An occasional silvery green Russian olive bush adds variety to the profile. Native species of willow, red-osier dogwood, and black hawthorne occur here. Red-winged blackbirds and yellow-headed blackbirds perch on cattail stalks and announce their territorial claims. Coots dabble and dive, clucking busily as they feed their young and watch for predators. Ruddy ducks and others, some of the twenty-one species of ducks known to nest or pass through, are equally engrossed in feeding. Although this is a protected area, the ducks are shy, and the visitor is wise to approach quietly and with binoculars.

At 1.2 miles you pass a 30-acre lake and a marsh of hardstem bulrush and cattails with some open water. Black terns swoop and flit overhead in flight patterns reminiscent of swallows. At 2.3 miles stop for a short hike to the Kepple Lake overlook. Much of the lake is visible from the road, but the walk provides a different perspective on the wildlife.

At about 4.4 miles stop for a boardwalk and an observation platform on the west side of Blackhorse Lake. The boardwalk is wheelchair-accessible and makes a short loop of about 0.15 mile. The air is alive with bird sounds: clicks, warbles, chirps, and the harsh *kraack!* of yellow-headed blackbirds. Then it's back to the car for the final bit past Swan Pond and the end of the tour.

There are several walking trails within the refuge, all of them with some wetland contact, but only the trail around Middle Pine Lake is primarily a wetland experience. It is a short but interesting walk. The trail begins across the street from the comfort station, cuts down a rocky hillside, and passes along the edge of Winslow Pool. Cross a dike between Winslow Pool and Middle Pine Lake, and follow the trail up to a rocky bluff overlooking the lake. Now is the time to get out the binoculars and bird book and start checking species. The lake is surrounded by hardstem bulrush and cattails and has floating masses of aquatic vegetation so thick that yellow-headed blackbirds land and peck for insects.

Mother ducks and their young plow their way through the green goo, and black terns swoop continuously overhead.

Black terns come to this area to breed, and their summer coloring is all dark except under the tail. With a slightly forked tail they might be confused with swallows except for their somewhat larger size. They build their nests on floating plant debris in cattail or bulrush marshes and lay two or three eggs. Their incessant activity, from constant patrolling to continual insect hunting and occasional plunging into the water for fish, makes them interesting to watch. Sometimes they are seen on Puget Sound in the fall.

Continue on as the trail passes tiny Ice Pond, nearly screened from view by tall cattails, and moves into open ponderosa pine forest, where you may see a doe feeding. This area has an understory of serviceberry,

Arrowhead and rushes at Turnbull

red-osier dogwood, and rose shrubs. Here you might see or hear the
Western wood-peewee, the pygmy nuthatch, Cassin's finch, or a red
crossbill, all birds typical of dry coniferous forests. At the top of the hill
a left turn takes you to the headquarters building; go right to get back
to the Winslow.

Here views of the pond are obscured by the bulrush and cattails, but
a careful listener will hear ducks going about their business on the other
side of the vegetation. The trail continues around the end of the lake and
offers a few small windows where one can see the water. In addition to
the Canada goose, mallard, blue-winged and green-winged teal, redhead
and ruddy duck, one might see a pair of trumpeter swans and migrating tundra swans. It is also possible to see sora, Virginia rail, common
snipe, spotted sandpiper, and the common yellowthroat. Using Turnbull
as a stopping point for spring and fall migrations, many birds move
through the area. The end of the trail forges through tall grass before
climbing back up the dry hill to the parking lot, where magpies sit in
the trees and watch impassively and squirrels scold vigorously and
shrilly.

24

West Hylebos State Park

Community: Forested swamp, bog
Size: 100 acres
Ownership: Washington State Parks Department
Season: Open all year
Cautions: No dogs, no bikes
Facilities: Latrine, maps, boardwalk, interpretive signs
Fee: None
Hours: 8:00 A.M. to dusk
Maps: Local
Highlights: Bog, huge old spruce trees, skunk cabbage, ferns
Nearest Town: Federal Way

From Federal Way take I-5 south of Federal Way to exit 142B. Go west
on South 348th Street approximately 1 mile, and turn left on 4th Avenue
South, a small dead-end road. Drive past several houses, and turn left
into the graveled parking lot. Maps are available at the bulletin board.

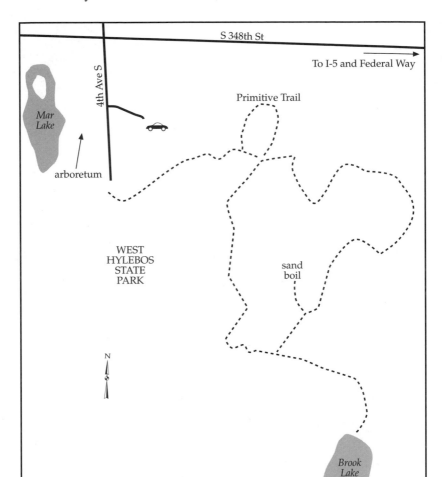

A haven of green sanity in the very center of urban "civilization"—and a gift to the state from the Marckx family. The main boardwalk is a loop of about 1 mile. Short side trips add about 0.5 mile to the total. The majority of the walk passes through typical forested swamp. Huge spruce and red cedar dominate the canopy. The larger specimens are over 500 years old. Wind storms in 1990 and 1993 brought down some of the giants and necessitated rebuilding portions of the boardwalk, but new tree seedlings are already crowded in the bare soil at the base of each uprooted tree.

Deciduous trees are an important component of this community. Alder, bitter cherry, and craggy old crab apples shade a thicket of shrubs. Cottonwood and Oregon ash are present but less common. If not for the boardwalk, most of the area would be almost inaccessible, so tangled and dense are the stands of salmonberry, elderberry, blackberries (native and imported), hardhack, and Indian plum. Below the shrubs sprout the giant leaves of skunk cabbage and the luxuriant fronds of lady fern. A carpet of false lily-of-the-valley covers any bare spot of ground left.

Swamp sparrow

Within the first quarter-mile or so, the boardwalk passes a deep sinkhole and the remnants of a bog. Acid-loving Labrador tea can be found here, with a lot of mosses. The area is on the dry side and supports a fine stand of hemlock trees; no sundews are found here.

About two-thirds of the way around the loop, the boardwalk branches. Go left for a short walk over a bridge (mucky, oozy below, with ferns and skunk cabbage) to small Brook Lake. Ducks dabble, herons fish, and dragonflies hunt here. There is a small observation platform and a muddy little path right to the lake edge. Backtrack and finish the walk, watching for the well-pecked rotting snag.

Don't neglect the side trips; the Primitive Trail leads into the swamp to a fine old spruce tree. One short side spur leads to a sand boil that is active fall through spring. The sand boil is the site of an artesian spring that sends water up with such force that it makes the sandy bottom boil with activity. Also worth a visit is a small arboretum south of the last house on 4th Avenue South that contains representatives of all the state's conifers, as well as Mar Lake, just to the west, which is home to numerous mallards.

Ferns of the understory at West Hylebos State Park

25

WILLAPA NATIONAL WILDLIFE REFUGE
Leadbetter Point

Community: Salt marsh, eelgrass beds, forested swamp
Size: 1,500 acres
Ownership: U.S. Department of the Interior, Fish and Wildlife
  Service
Season: Open year-round; some areas closed seasonally for wildlife
Cautions: Foot travel only; no camping, no fires, no collecting of
  artifacts
Facilities: Latrine, site map, camping and resorts to the south on
  the peninsula
Fee: None
Hours: Day use only
Maps: Local
Highlights: Migratory birds, wintering birds, pickleweed beds,
  spruce trees
Nearest Town: Oysterville

From Ilwaco take Highway 101 north; just 0.5 mile south of Seaview turn
onto Sandridge Road. There is a large refuge sign at the intersection.
Follow the road to the end, about 15 miles; then follow refuge signs to
Stackpole Road, and continue north to the end. If you need gas or food,
follow Highway 101 into Seaview and turn right (north) onto Highway
103, which will take you to Stackpole Road.

  Call the refuge headquarters for current information on what birds are
present; in fall and spring you can find large numbers of migrating
waterfowl and shorebirds. Their stay is brief but intense, and the sight of
thousands of birds flocking and feeding over the tide flats is one to remember. Winter is also an excellent time to visit, as large flocks of brant, Canada
geese, and several duck species overwinter in Willapa Bay. Once you arrive, the first order of business is to stroll down to the beach and have a
good look around. Great blue heron, year-round residents, pose like solitary sentinels; what other birds are present depends on the season.

  Next, turn left and follow the beach north. The trail goes through salt
marsh all the way to the sand dunes on the tip; then it cuts west across
the point to the ocean. At about 0.5 mile look for the first of the extensive

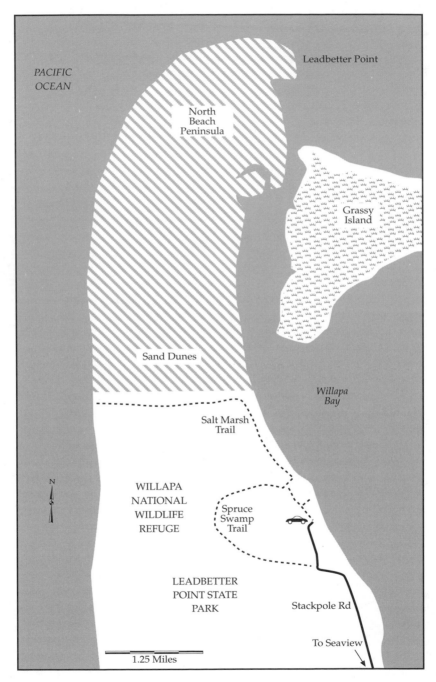

PACIFIC
OCEAN

Leadbetter Point

North
Beach
Peninsula

Grassy
Island

Sand Dunes

Willapa
Bay

Salt Marsh
Trail

WILLAPA
NATIONAL
WILDLIFE
REFUGE

Spruce
Swamp
Trail

N

LEADBETTER
POINT STATE
PARK

Stackpole Rd

To Seaview

1.25 Miles

Mud flats at Leadbetter Point

pickleweed beds. Some are being invaded rather heavily by cordgrass; others, perhaps a little drier, are holding their own. Mixed in with the pickleweed are a variety of other salt marsh species: another succulent, fleshy jaumea, as well as sea arrow-grass, seaside plantain, gumweed, and orache. Much of the pickleweed is wrapped in threads of gold—the parasitic dodder. Saltgrass, although present, is not nearly as common as in some of the other salt marshes described in this book. And everywhere you look, round patches of cordgrass march farther and farther into the bay, foreshadowing the future as they crowd out native vegetation.

The northern tip—the "point" in Leadbetter Point—is closed from April through August to protect nesting snowy plovers, one of the many sandpiper species. Snowy plover numbers have been greatly reduced by human disturbance. They nest in a simple scrape in the sand, and when scared off the nest by the unwitting walker (the birds are perfectly camouflaged for sandy beaches), their eggs or chicks are extremely vulnerable.

After salt marsh walking and bird-watching, turn around and walk back along the beach. About where the salt marsh starts is a sign indicating a trail inland. Walk for perhaps 0.1 mile to the main trail, a wide path in the sand dunes. Lodgepole pine and kinnikinnick predominate, but another import, gorse, is in great evidence and is armed with vicious spines. Follow the trail marked "loop"; it leads into the heart of the peninsula and eventually into a swampy spruce forest. Cover yourself with gobs of mosquito repellent and then admire the elegant spruces with their massive straight trunks and characteristic flaky gray bark. The understory is a jungle of greenery; most common are sedges and ferns. The trail loops back to the road, emerging at the boundary of the refuge and Leadbetter Point State Park, a largely undeveloped natural area. Turn left and walk the road for 0.75 mile to reach the parking lot.

Another resting site for migratory waterfowl is Dungeness Wildlife Area. It has the longest sand spit in the state, and it also has thousands of flocking birds, as well as a salt lagoon.

Salt marsh and lodgepole pine in the sand dunes at Willapa Bay

3
WETLAND PLANTS
AND ANIMALS

Forested Swamp

WETLAND PLANTS AND ANIMALS

SENSITIVE AND ENDANGERED PLANTS _____

A few plants associated with wetlands are on the sensitive or endangered list for Washington. Some have been collected or noted in specific areas; others have not been seen for years and may be extinct. These are plants commonly found in bogs; the only three exceptions are water-hemlock, water lobelia, and hooded ladies' tresses.

There are two orchids: Hooded ladies' tresses (*Spiranthes romanzoffiana*) flowers in a distinctive spiral form; three-quarter-inch long greenish white flowers spiral upward in one of four rows. Flowers resemble a hooded tube with a tongue sticking out; the stalk may grow 2 feet tall in moist and swampy areas. Last collected in Washington in 1912, Choriso bog orchid (*Habenaria chorisiana*) bears tiny greenish flowers on a 5-inch plant, with two or three elongated oval basal leaves.

Two members of the sunflower family are on the sensitive list. Common apargidium (*Apargidium boreale*) has only yellow ray flowers. Ray flowers and disk flowers are found in the sunflower family; ray flowers are strap-shaped petals such as those found on the daisy. Disk flowers are the tiny flowers packed together in the center, forming a button. The solitary head is shaped like a badminton shuttlecock; all leaves are basal (attached at the base), elongated, and tapering to a point. Rush aster (*Aster junciformis*) bears pale blue ray flowers and narrow leaves.

Brook lobelia (*Lobelia kalmii*) is blue with a white eye and spatula-shaped basal leaves; it may be extinct. Water lobelia (*Lobelia dortmanna*) is considered sensitive; white flowers form a tube with five back-curved petals on this aquatic perennial found growing along pond margins. Another pond-edge plant is bulblet-bearing water-hemlock (*Cicuta bulbifera*), a highly toxic member of the parsley family, with greenish white flowers.

Menzies' burnet (*Sanguisorba menziesii*) is at the limit of its range in the Olympic Peninsula. It has no petals, but its sepals are purple and form a round head. Bog clubmoss (*Lycopodium inundatum*), another unusual plant, looks much like a very large moss. Alaska plantain (*Plantago macrocarpa*), similar to our garden weed, bears tiny flowers packed together into a dense, cylindric head. It is commonly found in British Columbia but is disappearing from the southern part of its distribution in the state of Washington.

The Douglas gentian (*Gentiana douglasiana*) produces greenish petals with two teeth on each lobe and has nearly been collected to death. Another unusual flower is produced by fringed grass-of-parnassus (*Parnassia fimbriata* var. *kotzebuei*). The showy white petals are fringed at the base and have five veins, all borne above heart-shaped leaves.

BOG PLANTS
Sphagnum, also known as peat moss, is the prime indicator plant of a bog. Sphagnum leaves are a single cell layer thick, with large clear dead cells alternating with smaller living cells. A tiny pore opens into the dead cell, allowing water into the space; this moss can hold up to twenty times its dry weight in water. Sphagnum bogs are very specialized, nutrient-poor habitats that remain unchanged for centuries.

Sundews (*Drosera* spp.) are carnivorous bog plants that supplement their diet by digesting insects. Gland-bearing hairs along the leaves secretes drops of sticky fluid that are attractive to insects. When an insect touches the leaf, the entire leaf rolls inward and special enzymes digest the insect. Both long-leaved sundew (*Drosera anglica*) and round-leaved sundew (*D. rotundifolia*) are found here. Another insectivorous plant, butterwort (*Pinguicula vulgaris*), catches and digests its prey with a shiny mucilage on the surface of the leaves. It is related to the aquatic bladderwort. Solitary lavender flowers are borne on leafless stems and have a saclike extension to the rear.

Tall white bog orchid (*Habenaria dilatata*) grows 3 feet tall and has five to thirty fragrant white flowers spiraling up from the base. Roundleaf bog orchid (*H. orbiculata*), commonly found at the edges of cold mountain streams and bogs, has greenish white flowers and a leafless stem.

Northern starflower (*Trientalis arctica*) has white starlike flowers borne on slender stems. A member of the primrose family, starflower grows only in bogs and swampy areas.

The many-stemmed swamp gentian (*Gentiana sceptrum*) bears deep blue flowers with dark green speckles inside. It is found in coastal bogs along with the buckbean (*Menyanthes trifoliata*). Numerous flowers are crowded together at the end of a foot-long stalk with basal, trifoliate leaves on long stems. The fused tubular petals have lobes covered with a fringe.

Few-flowered spikerush (*Eleocharis pauciflora*) possesses compressed or angular stems, with a spikelet borne at the end of the stem, that bend and catch on moist ground. These root to produce more rhizomes and new plants. Found around the world in northern latitudes, this plant

Sedge

tolerates both salty and alkaline conditions. Cottongrass (*Eriophorum* spp.) is a common inhabitant of bogs. White bristles surround the seed, creating a cottony tuft at the end of the flowering stalk.

Several shrubs can be found in bogs. Cranberry (*Vaccinium* spp.) is a creeping woody plant with shiny green leaves. The supermarket escapee, large cranberry, is evergreen, but the native cranberry is small and deciduous and has rolled-under leaf margins. Swamp laurel (*Kalmia polifolia*) has delicate flower buds and rose pink blossoms. Two varieties of swamp laurel, lowland and montane, hybridize when their ranges overlap. Both have evergreen leaves, dark green and glossy on top, white and granular beneath with the leaf margins slightly rolled down around the edges. Another shrub with evergreen leaves is Labrador tea (*Ledum groenlandicum*). Slightly resembling a rhododendron, the leaves are distinguished by rusty hairs covering the underside. A related species has been used to brew aromatic trapper's tea. It should be consumed in moderation because it contains toxic alkaloids.

EELGRASS BED PLANTS

The dominant plant in this community is eelgrass (*Zostera* spp.). Exposed only during low tides, it forms an underwater forest rooted in the mud of the tide flat. *Zostera marina* is the larger and most common of our two species of eelgrass. Its branching stems can be as much as 8 feet long, with strap-shaped leaves up to a half-inch wide. It often forms windrows on the beach after being dropped by the receding tide, and it

provides dinner for beach fleas. Flowers are contained in a swollen structure much like a compressed pea pod.

Wigeon grass (*Ruppia maritima*), also known as ditch grass, is a submerged perennial with round stems and threadlike leaves up to 8 inches
long. The flowers are tiny and inconspicuous, but the fruits are borne
on a slender stalk that elongates and coils into a spiral as it matures, often to a foot long. Wigeon grass is a favorite food of migrating waterfowl. It grows in quiet waters along the coast and in brackish or saline
sloughs and ponds.

FORESTED SWAMP PLANTS

Western red cedar (*Thuja plicata*) is one of the primary species in this
community. An elegant, pyramid-shaped tree, it is one of our slowest-
growing conifers. With a fluted and buttressed trunk, it has fibrous
reddish-brown bark easily stripped off in narrow shreds. The resinous
wood is naturally resistant to rot. Two other conifers are present in varying degrees in wetlands. Sitka spruce (*Picea sitchensis*) is most common
on the west edge of the Olympic Peninsula. It is easily identified by its
scaly, smooth gray bark and by its sharply pointed needles. Hemlock
(*Tsuga heterophylla*) is not primarily a wetland species, but it is tolerant
of shade and grows best on moist, acid soils. It is common in drier
swamps, where the water table is not high year-round. Hemlock has
delicate foliage and a drooping top. Each dark-green needle has two
white bands on the underside.

The common red alder (*Alnus rubra*) has dark-green egg-shaped
leaves with toothed edges, and a smooth gray trunk. Unlike most deciduous trees, it has leaves that are still green when they fall. Oregon ash
(*Fraxinus latifolia*) and cottonwood (*Populus trichocarpa*) both have high
tolerance for submersion. Ash has leaves up to 12 inches long that are
subdivided into oblong leaflets, and thick, furrowed bark. The fruits have
a single papery wing and hang in dense clusters. Cottonwoods are
rough-barked trees with shiny buds that are sweetly aromatic in spring.
The triangular leaves are green above and silvery white below.

Bigleaf maple (*Acer macrophyllum*) is our largest maple and has the
largest leaves of all maple species. The leaves have five deep lobes with
thickened middle veins. The bark is brown, furrowed into small plates,
and frequently covered with moss, lichens, and even ferns. Bigleaf maple
flowers early in the spring, with long clusters of small greenish yellow
flowers, and is an important early nectar source. Vine maple (*Acer
circinatum*) is a much smaller tree, with long, sprawling branches and

smooth bright-green bark. Small leaves have seven to eleven sharply pointed lobes. Clusters of tiny red flowers appear in spring, later forming paired fruits with "helicopter" wings. Douglas maple (*Acer douglasii*) is more common east of the Cascades. Its leaves have three sharply pointed lobes.

A great variety of shrubby species may be present in the understory. Red-osier dogwood (*Cornus stolonifera*) has bright red twigs that lend color to winter thickets. The leaves are textured, with five to seven parallel veins that converge at the tip. The small white flowers have four petals and are in open clusters. Crab apple (*Pyrus fusca*) bears sour but edible small apples. It has long, toothed leaves and deeply fissured bark. This tree reproduces rapidly by suckers from the base.

The ferocious devil's club (*Oplopanax horridum*) grows along streams and in seepage areas from the lowlands to fairly high elevations, mostly west of the Cascades. Springy stems grow up to 12 feet tall and are covered with spines. Bold maplelike leaves and bright red berries identify it late in summer. The densely clustered flowers are greenish white.

Another thorny species, although not nearly as vicious, is the salmonberry (*Rubus spectabilis*). Its bright magenta flowers become succulent, salmon-colored orange berries. The shiny brown stems are around 6 feet high; they often form dense thickets.

Ferns are common understory inhabitants. Lady fern (*Athyrium felix-femina*) is most often encountered, with fronds up to 6 feet long, widest in the middle and tapering at both ends. The leaves are finely divided and have a lacelike appearance. Deer fern (*Blechnum spicant*) replaces lady fern in coastal swamps and is abundant along the Ahlstroms Prairie to Lake Ozette trail. Deer fern has two entirely different kinds of leaves. The basal leaves are divided into bars. A few leaves arising from the center of the crown are taller with very slender leaflets and dry out in late summer. These special leaves are the only ones that produce spores. Maidenhair fern (*Adiantum pedatum*) has black stems and large, delicately scalloped, airy leaflets.

Touch-me-not (*Impatiens noli-tangere*) is sometimes called jewelweed because of its distinctive bright orange flowers. The flowers develop into elongated pods that explode when touched, propelling the seeds out into the landscape. Jewelweed may form dense stands at the edges of shallow freshwater marshes and can also be found under alders. It is common at the Skagit Wildlife Area.

Occasionally the understory of a forested swamp will be rather bare and dominated by only one or two species, usually skunk cabbage

(*Lysichitum americanum*) and slough sedge (*Carex obnupta*), a large, coarse-leaved sedge. The large, bright-yellow flowers of skunk cabbage are indicators both of spring and of a wetland. The odor is skunklike but not offensively so. The leaves and roots of skunk cabbage are eaten by bear, and deer browse on the leaves. The roots, when boiled, are edible; Native Americans utilized them, although they did not consider them a delicacy.

FRESHWATER MARSH PLANTS

Vegetation in a freshwater marsh tends to fall into several zones. Edge plants live in highly saturated soil, although there may not be standing water here. Emergent water plants are those rooted underwater but largely living above the surface. Floating plants form a zone farther out in the water. A few are free-floating, but most are rooted. Finally, submersed plants often produce huge beds a much greater distance from the shore and provide aquatic organisms with food, shelter, and nest-building materials. When this organic material is deposited, it decreases the depth of the water and adds to the filling-in of the marsh.

There are many plants that grow on soil that is not always below the surface of the water. Sweetgale (*Myrica gale*) is easily recognized by the bright yellow wax glands that dot the leaves and by its sweet scent. Flowers are in catkins of stacked brown scales that appear before the leaves in the spring. The lance-shaped leaves have a rounded tip. Growing on slightly drier land, Douglas spirea (*Spiraea douglasii*) can be spotted by its fuzzy pink flower heads. Sometimes reaching 6 feet high, the simple leaves are dark green on top and much paler beneath. Leaf edges are toothed toward the end and entire nearest the stem. This shrub often rings a lake or marsh, contributing to the growth of solid land.

The marsh cinquefoil (*Potentilla palustris*) has reddish stems nearly 3 feet long and purple flowers. Pinnate leaves have five to seven light-green leaflets. Forget-me-not (*Myosotis* spp.) annuals bear flowers on long, coiled stalks that uncoil and elongate as the plant matures. The flower begins as a blue funnel with five abruptly spreading lobes; with age the color changes to pink. Marsh forget-me-not (*Myosotis scorpioides*) stems lie on the ground; its flowers are tiny. Woods forget-me-not (*M. sylvatica*) is the escaped cultivar, with blue flowers. Small-flowered forget-me-not (*M. laxa*) is common in open areas, ditches, and swamps.

Dwarf St. John's wort (*Hypericum anagalloides*) forms dense mats from stems lying along the ground. Tiny oval leaves are opposite, with oil glands appearing as dark dots. The coppery yellow flowers are only a quarter-inch long.

Yellow pond lily

Because of the presence of silica in the cell walls of the horsetail, this plant is also called scouring rush. Water horsetail (*Equisetum fluviatile*) grows to 3 feet tall with hollow, grooved stems. The joints are green with sharp black teeth. Some have no branches, while others have many, bright green and wirelike, arising in whorls from the joints.

Bugleweed lacks the typical "minty" scent of the mint family. Small white flowers are bunched in leaf axils. Northern bugleweed (*Lycopus uniflora*) stems are unbranched, bearing opposite, coarsely toothed, hairy leaves. Rough bugleweed (*L. asper*) is taller than northern and has branched stems and tiny white flowers. It is found only east of the Cascades.

Frequently mistaken for western water-hemlock, water parsley (*Oenanthe sarmentosa*) is probably a poisonous plant. The twice pinnately compound leaves have toothed leaflets, and leaflet veins run directly to the tips of the teeth. Succulent, reclining stems root at the nodes; they are viney and often a reddish color. Umbels of tiny greenish white flowers have a faint, pleasant scent. They are borne laterally in flat-topped clusters.

A white flower with the lower petals bearing thin purple lines distinguishes the small white violet (*Viola macloskeyi*). The 2½-inch-tall plant has a single flower and heart-shaped leaves. Fruit is in an angular capsule that explodes when mature. Violets also produce flowers that set seed without ever opening.

Moving into the marsh zone with more water, we find a number of the sedges, a huge family of grasslike plants with triangular stems. Their flowers are reduced and wind-pollinated and are borne in spikes. The stems are usually triangular. Common sedges in this community include California sedge (*Carex californica*), hoary sedge (*C. canescens*), shore sedge (*C. lenticularis*), and water sedge (*C. aquatilis*).

Two bulrushes are commonly found in this community. The American threesquare (*Scirpus americanus*) has triangular stems scattered along the rhizomes. The flowers are stalkless in a tight cluster below the top of the plants. It is one of the most widespread flowering plants, occuring on several continents. Hardstem bulrush (*S. acutus*) is the giant, growing 6 feet tall. The stems are round and olive green and can be as large as 1½ inches at the base. Hardstem is commonly associated with cattails in shallow marshes and with white water lilies in deep marshes. It can form exclusionary single-species stands and is able to grow in water up to 3 feet deep.

Giant bur-reed (*Sparganium eurycarpum*) is a distinctive perennial, up to 4 feet tall, with separate male and female flower clusters that look like green prickly balls. Both male and female burs are borne vertically on a stalk. The keeled light-green leaves are soft and spongy, triangular in cross-section. Growing in the same general habitat, yellow iris (*Iris pseudacorus*) has bright yellow flowers with purple penciling. Growing 4 feet tall in dense clumps at the edge of water, iris is an introduced European species.

The water-plantain family provides two plants to this community. Broad-leaved arrowhead (*Sagittaria latifolia*) grows on the west side of the Cascades and northern arrowhead (*S. cuneata*) on the east side. Both plants have showy white flowers an inch across and large arrowhead-shaped leaves. The starchy tubers, called wapato, were an important food source for Native Americans. Broadleaf water-plantain (*Alisma plantago-aquatica*) is the most common water-plantain. Tiny flowers with pink petals are in airy bunches at the end of the flowers' stalk, much like baby's breath. Oblong leaves rise from the base.

Cattail (*Typha latifolia*) is our most familiar indicator of wetlands, since it dominates acres of marsh land. The broad, strap-shaped leaves may grow to 5 feet, and the flower stalk extends a foot above them. The root-stock is high in starch and makes excellent eating. The cylindrical flower head has male flowers along the top of the stalk, below which the female flowers are packed into the familiar brown velvety "tail." Tiny hairs surrounding the seeds help them float away on wind and water.

Western water-hemlock (*Cicuta douglasii*) is reported to be the most toxic plant in the temperate zone. Reports of human deaths after consumption are not uncommon. All parts are poisonous, but the toxin is concentrated in the roots and stems. Single-stemmed and 8 feet tall, it has leaves that are pinnately compound and greenish white flowers that are carrotlike. The roots have cross-partitions that form distinct chambers which can be seen when cut lengthwise.

Marsh arrow-grass (*Triglochin palustre*) has thick, basal rushlike leaves with round stems. Growing up to 2 feet tall, the small greenish flowers are in a spikelike arrangement. Growing slightly lower in the marsh is mare's tail (*Hippuris vulgaris*), with partly emergent stems a foot high growing from creeping rhizomes. It looks like a large green feather. Whorled leaves are linear and stalkless. Inconspicuous flowers occur in the whorls of the upper leaves.

Purple loosestrife (*Lythrum salicaria*) was introduced in Washington in the 1920s. Reaching 10 feet tall, it is covered with striking purple flowers on a long upright stalk in late summer. The opposite leaves are willowlike, attached directly to a four-sided main stalk. It outcompetes cattail and soon establishes uniform stands in place of the cattail. Some of the potholes in Frenchman Hills illustrate this behavior. The roots quickly form a dense mat and are very hard to pull.

Aquatic smartweed (*Polygonum amphibium*) grows in wet soil or shallow water. Bright pink flowers in terminal spikes sometimes form a floating lens-shaped patch of color. The stalked alternate leaves are elliptic with smooth margins and pointed tips.

Rooted but floating plants include the water lilies, the pondweeds (a huge group), and the water shield. The native yellow water lily (*Nuphar polysepalum*) has bold yellow, globular flowers. The leaves have upturned edges and are often held slightly above the water. It requires a marsh 3 to 8 feet deep. The fragrant white water lily (*Nymphaea odorata*) has many-petaled flowers and leaves that float flat on the water. It has been introduced here. The pondweeds (*Potamogeton* spp.) have 1,000 species worldwide, with twenty common in our area. Floating-leaved pondweed (*P. natans*) has egg-shaped floating leaves and linear submerged leaves. Grass-leaved pondweed (*P. gramineus*) has oblong floating leaves and finely divided submerged leaves. Richardson's pondweed (*P. richardsonii*) has only submerged leaves, all straplike. The stems of pondweeds are always submerged and seem to fill the shallow pond edges up to 10 feet deep. Water shield (*Brasenia schreberi*) carries its shield-shaped leaves just under the surface of the water. A gelatinous covering on its leaves and stems is the identifying trait.

Water starwort (*Callitriche heterophylla*) is inconspicuous but common. Often submerged, it is occasionally found rooting in shallow pond edges or lying on mud surfaces. The submerged leaves are linear, the upper leaves egg-shaped. Tiny flowers are borne in the leaf axils.

Duckweed (*Lemna minor*) floats on the surface of the water. The plants are rarely found in flower and reproduce vegetatively. Often these plants multiply enough to totally cover the surface of the water, and then they provide a landing platform for insects looking for a place to drink water. The leaves are oval with three veins and have a single inch-long root. They look like large green yeast budding on the water's surface.

Eurasian water milfoil (*Myriophyllum spicatum*) has a featherlike appearance because of its finely branching submersed leaves. The upper leaves and stem may be pink, and the mature leaves are in whorls of four. Minute white flowers are borne on leafless spikes projecting above the water's surface. Introduced in the state about 1977, water milfoil has spread rapidly through vegetative fragments. Efforts to control the plant have had little impact. Tolerant of brackish water, it can also invade coastal streams and bays.

Three species of bladderwort (*Utricularia* spp.) grow in our range. The leaves of these highly specialized aquatic plants have small, asymmetrical bladders with mouthlike openings. Trigger hairs on the outside of the bladder cause it to contract, often sucking small invertebrates into the enclosure. Internal hairlike cells prevent the animals' escape until they are digested by the plant. The common bladderwort (*U. vulgaris*) has coarse alternate leaves that are two-parted at the base and then repeatedly and unequally divided. It has up to twenty yellow snapdragonlike flowers on stalks that extend above the water's surface like small periscopes.

Several buttercups (*Ranunculus* spp.) occur in shallow water. Pond buttercup (*R. subrigidus*) has finely dissected leaves that do not collapse when the plant is lifted from the water. The flower stalks are leafless and tend to curve when in fruit. It has white petals. White water buttercup

(*R. aquatilis*) is specialized for shallow ponds, with submerged leaves that are reduced to threadlike structures, and floating leaves with three-lobed blades. Yellow water buttercup (*R. flabellaris*) may grow totally underwater. A perennial with a hollow, branching stem, it roots at the nodes. It is restricted to east of the Cascades.

SALT MARSH PLANTS

Plants in salt marshes tend to be low-growing. One of the tallest is salt marsh cordgrass (*Spartina alterniflora*), which is often over 3 feet tall. Sturdy rhizomes allow this plant to form dense stands that initially appear as small round islands on mud flats. Tough 1-inch leaves fold inward at the tip. Cordgrass is a dominant marsh plant along the Atlantic and came to Willapa Bay in the late 1800s as a packing material for oysters from the East Coast. It has changed the pattern of water circulation and silt deposition, with a consequent shift of tideflats to salt marsh. These changes have influenced the invertebrate food supply of migratory birds and the feeding and nursery areas for fish. Much of the bay has become unsuitable for oyster growing. The cordgrass seems to spread by rhizome rather than by seed germination. Cordgrass removes excess salt from its tissues by excreting it through modified stem cells and depositing it on the stem surface, where it is seen as tiny light-reflecting crystals.

Saltgrass (*Distichlis spicata*) is a rigid-stemmed grass that may become 16 inches tall. Dense colonies form from vigorous creeping rhizomes. The stiff, two-ranked leaves are numerous and distinctive. Saltgrass can also excrete excessive salt. Alkali grass (*Puccinellia* spp.) is another tufted perennial with hollow stems and rolled leaves. Several species are found here.

Higher up on the beach, large-headed sedge (*Carex macrocephala*) occurs on sandy beaches and dunes. The leaves are clustered at the base, fairly wide and yellowish green with a distinct channel. The flower head is egg-shaped and up to 4 inches long. Low bulrush (*Scirpus cernuus*) is the only annual bulrush in the Pacific Northwest. While it can be found in freshwater marshes, it is more common in salt marshes. Its numerous slender stems may grow 8 inches high. The spikelets are solitary and near the tip of the stem. Lyngbye's sedge (*Carex lyngbyei*) is salt-tolerant and grows lushly in the high intertidal marsh where there is fresh water input. It forms great even-shaped hummocks in the marsh, giving a distinctive character to this low-lying land. Slough sedge (*C. obnupta*) is a similar plant, growing up to 3 feet high. It is most common in coastal swamps.

Shooting star

Superficially similar to a grass, seaside arrow-grass (*Triglochin maritimum*) has short, sturdy rhizomes that produce tufts of half-round basal leaves. The small greenish flowers are borne on a narrow spike. It grows in alkaline as well as saline areas. Found in a similar habitat, seaside plantain (*Plantago maritima*) has leaves that are long and narrow and tiny flowers packed together into dense cylindrical heads.

With a golden-yellow, buttercuplike flower, Pacific silverweed (*Potentilla pacifica*) has leaves and flower stems that form a rosette at the top of the root. The pinnately compound leaves, each with eleven to twenty-one leaflets, are a shiny dark green on top and a silky white below. Long runners spread out from the base of the plant, rooting at the nodes. Seaside buttercup (*Ranunculus cymbalaris*) has heart-shaped leaves with scalloped margins borne on long stems. Growing 1 foot tall, it bears pale yellow flowers. Another plant with yellow flowers, gumweed (*Grindelia integrifolia*), is recognized by it sticky, resin-dotted leaves. The yellow flowers are surrounded by very gummy bracts that have long, slender, spreading tips, giving a burlike appearance to the flower buds.

Orache (*Atriplex patula*) is not restricted to wetlands but also grows inland on alkaline soils. The triangular upper leaves and a frosty appearance distinguish it. Tiny greenish flowers are crowded together in spikes.

Two plants from the sunflower family that are often confused are brass buttons (*Cotula coronopifolia*) and fleshy jaumea (*Jaumea carnosa*). Both may live very low in the salt marsh, often being inundated by the tide. Brass buttons, introduced from South Africa, has alternate, stalkless oblong leaves; jaumea has opposite leaves. Both have solitary heads of flowers; brass buttons has only disk flowers and no rays, while jaumea has disk flowers with small, narrow ray flowers. Both may form exclusionary stands above and below the tide level.

Glasswort (*Salicornia virginica*) is a round, fleshy perennial with stems up to 3 feet long, usually lying on the ground. The leaves are reduced to tiny scales, and tiny flowers occur in sunken pits on the ends of the stems. This is one of the few plants that can tolerate the high levels of salt found around salt lagoons, such as Jackle's Lagoons at American Camp on San Juan Island. Many people eat this plant, also called pickleweed, either preserved or fresh. An associated plant found growing on glasswort, salt marsh dodder (*Cuscuta salina*), is a parasitic plant with tiny bell-shaped flowers. Consisting of threadlike delicate stems that wind and twine on its host and surrounding plants, it produces a vivid golden-brown web on the landscape. Since it does not manufacture its own food, it does not exhibit the green presence of chlorophyll.

WET MEADOW PLANTS

Rushes are indicator plants for wet meadows. These grasslike plants have unjointed round stems growing in dense tufts. Common rush (*Juncus effusus*) grows in moist areas from coastal tideflats into mountain meadows. The 4-inch-tall Baltic rush (*J. balticus*) is often found in low pastures, marshes, and pond edges. It has brown, papery flowers that squeeze out near the top third of the stem.

Reed canarygrass (*Phalaris arundinaceae*) dominates the landscape, growing up to 7 feet tall. The terminal flower spike is 6 inches long; our only other tall grass, reed grass, has bolder leaves and a feathery, purplish flower spike—it tends to need more standing water, although it is seen in ditches along roads.

Shrub and tree species often invade wet meadows. Red alder (*Alnus rubra*) is an opportunistic species, not limited to wetlands. It is easily identified by its large, egg-shaped leaves with saw-toothed, rolled-under margins. Alder has bacterial nodules on its roots that convert atmospheric nitrogen to a form utilized for plant growth; it functions much like legumes in enriching the soil. Another woody inhabitant is the willow, which has simple, alternate leaves. Scouler's willow (*Salix scouleriana*) is our most common upland willow; because of frequent proximity to low-lying meadows, it may become established on drier areas of the meadow. Quaking aspen (*Populus tremuloides*) takes hold in wet areas—its silver trunks contrast with the round dark-green leaves, which respond to the slightest wind movement. Because the roots readily produce suckers, a single aspen soon turns into a grove of aspen, all waving bright gold leaves in the fall.

Skunk cabbage (*Lysichitum americanum*), more common in forested swamps, is often found scattered in very wet meadows. The bright-yellow flower is really a modified leaf that surrounds a fleshy flower spike. The other leaves develop after the plant flowers, and their 3-foot length makes them easy to spot in a field. Less readily seen from afar, creeping buttercup (*Ranunculus repens*) is especially common in wet meadows, often coming to dominate the landscape through runners that root at the stem nodes. When in bloom, the bright-yellow, five-petaled flowers transform a meadow with waves of color. Tall swamp onion

(*Allium validum*) is a member of the lily family with delicate pink flowers nodding on a stem. Its typical onion leaves produce an onion odor when crushed and differentiate this plant from death camas, which may grow in the same habitat.

The common monkeyflower (*Mimulus guttatus*) is not restricted to wet meadows but does require standing or seepage water up to middle elevations. It is an annual, growing 2 feet tall. Its fairly large yellow snapdragon flowers have an inflated lower lip with red markings. Associated with it are the veronicas, or speedwells. From the same family as the monkeyflower (figworts), the veronicas have four unequal flower lobes, the lower lobe the smallest. American speedwell (*Veronica americana*) is probably the most common; it has bright blue flowers. Thyme-leaved speedwell (*V. speryllifolia*) has smaller leaves and flowers, which could be blue or white. Mints, easily identified by their square stems, are also found in wet meadows. Skullcap (*Scutellaria galericulata*) is widely distributed and has pairs of blue flowers with white markings in each leaf axil.

Much more colorful than lowland wet meadows are the subalpine and alpine wet meadows. The short growing season and abundant moisture in montane environments result in an explosion of plant growth and flowering. Our largest lilies, two species of false hellebore, occur here. Green false hellebore (*Veratrum viride*) may be 7 feet tall. The huge young shoots resemble ears of corn but are poisonous to us. Its greenish yellow flowers are loosely clustered on drooping branches. California false hellebore (*V. californicum*) is slightly larger and has white, tightly packed flower spikes.

Another tall plant, Sitka valerian (*Valeriana sitchensis*), is a common sight on subalpine seepage slopes. The small white flowers, in terminal clusters, have a cloying, sweet scent; the stamens extend beyond the flower head, giving it a light, fluffy appearance. The slightly succulent leaves and stems have an unusual odor when crushed.

Chickweed monkeyflower (*Mimulus alsinoides*) is restricted to the montane environment. An annual, its yellow flowers have a large maroon blotch on the lower lip. Subalpine monkeyflower (*M. tilingii*) is found at higher elevations; primrose monkeyflower (*M. primuloides*) and floriferous monkeyflower (*M. floribundus*) grow east of the Cascade crest. Lewis's monkeyflower (*M. lewisii*) has pink flowers marked with yellow and grows in all our higher mountains. Another figwort, elephant's head lousewort (*Pedicularis groenlandica*), has purple blossoms, and its fused petals resemble an elephant's head.

The buttercup family is well represented in high wet meadows. Marsh marigolds (*Caltha* spp.) are common in wet depressions. White marsh marigold (*C. biflora*) has broad, rounded leaves and pale yellow flowers. Elkslip (*C. leptosepala*) has greenish flowers and oblong toothed leaves. Blooming just as the snow recedes, globeflower (*Trollius laxus*) looks like a buttercup with cream-colored flowers.

Shooting stars (*Dodecatheon* spp.) are eye-catching wildflowers, lighting up muddy depressions and seepage areas. The purple petals sweep back sharply away from the stamens, which are partially joined to form a tube. Alpine shooting star (*D. alpinum*) has narrow linear leaves and four petals. Jeffrey's shooting star (*D. jeffreyi*) has broader leaves and five petals. The explorer's gentian (*Gentiana calycosa*) is particularly beautiful with its petals and sepals fused to form a funnel-shapped vivid blue flower. Growing up to 2 feet tall, it flowers very late in the season.

Willows are common in montane meadows, as is subalpine spirea (*Spiraea densiflora*), looking much like its lowland cousin, hardhack. A twisted and stunted subalpine fir (*Abies lasiocarpa*) may be mixed in with the shrubs.

Although beautiful flowering plants are one of the attractions to alpine hiking, the most important and numerous plants are the grasses, sedges, and rushes. Black alpine sedge (*Carex nigricans*) is a short sedge with dark flowers, common in seepage areas and below melting snow banks. Cottongrasses (*Eriophorum* spp.) are also sedges; their fine white seed bristles elongate and look like cotton.

AMPHIBIANS

Amphibians were the first vertebrates adapted to life on land, and many amphibians are still closely tied to the aquatic lifestyle of their forebears, returning to rivers, lakes, or ponds to breed. The cool, moist climate of Washington is ideal for amphibians, and two groups, the salamanders and the frogs, are well represented here. Salamanders have slender bodies, long tails, and like-sized fore- and hind limbs. Frogs have compact tailless bodies and outsized hind legs. The greatest dangers to our native amphibians are people, imported fish species, and the imported bullfrog. Loss of wetland habitat has affected many amphibian species, and fish and bullfrogs have apparently eliminated native populations from some ponds and lakes.

Salamanders: Pond- and stream-breeding salamanders usually have a distinct aquatic larval stage and a terrestrial adult stage. Some salamanders retain the larval form as they become sexually mature, a phenomenon known as neoteny. Neoteny is quite common in permanent bodies of water and less common in seasonal waters. A giant "tadpole" sporting gills and small legs is not a tadpole at all but a neotenic salamander.

Both larval and adult salamanders are opportunistic carnivores. The most common prey is insects, but salamanders also eat snails, worms, crayfish, tadpoles, and even other salamanders. They are nocturnal creatures, and although little is known about predation on them, their major enemies are probably snakes, frogs, birds, and small mammals. Many salamander species are able to secrete poisons that make them unpalatable or even dangerous to consume.

There are three species of mole salamanders in Washington; the long-toed, the northwestern, and the tiger. All fairly large, they have prominent vertical creases along the sides of their bodies. The adults are rarely seen since they spend most of the year in burrows.

With the widest distribution, the long-toed salamander, dark with a yellow dorsal stripe, is found in most regions of the state, from sea level to around 6,000 feet. It commonly lays its eggs in temporary pools.

Moist brown, smooth skin characterizes the northwestern salamander. It is found along the Pacific Coast inland to just east of the Cascade crest below 6,000 feet. It lays its eggs in wetlands near ponds and slow streams. This is one of the few native amphibians able to survive in lowland waters that have populations of introduced fish and bullfrogs, possibly because both larvae and adults are mildly poisonous.

The tiger salamander, found in Washington only in the Columbia Basin and the northeast portion of the state, is the largest of the mole salamanders (up to 13 inches) and is distinctive with its olive blotches and black markings. Tiger larvae, known as "water dogs," are commonly sold as fish bait in eastern Washington.

The rough-skinned newt is distributed from the coast to the eastern foothills of the Cascades. It is the only salamander in our range that has rough, dry skin. In winter, breeding males change appearance, the skin becoming smooth and moist. Rough-skinned newts are brown above and bright orange below. They are very poisonous; human deaths from eating this newt have been reported. It lays its eggs in the vegetated fringes of permanent bodies of water.

Frogs: Frogs are the most successful group of amphibians, displaying a wide geographical and ecological distribution. The frog life cycle is a complex one, requiring some radical changes as the aquatic larval tadpole metamorphoses into the terrestrial adult frog. Most species

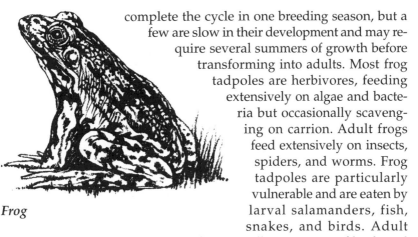

Frog

complete the cycle in one breeding season, but a few are slow in their development and may require several summers of growth before transforming into adults. Most frog tadpoles are herbivores, feeding extensively on algae and bacteria but occasionally scavenging on carrion. Adult frogs feed extensively on insects, spiders, and worms. Frog tadpoles are particularly vulnerable and are eaten by larval salamanders, fish, snakes, and birds. Adult frogs are also prey to fish and snakes as well as a variety of birds and mammals. Many adult frogs have poison glands that discourage some predators.

The Pacific treefrog is the most common and widely distributed frog in the state. This is our spring peeper; it announces the breeding season with persistent loud choruses. It commonly lays its eggs in shallow, vegetated, seasonal wetlands. Treefrogs have moist, smooth skin ranging in color from bright green to brown or gray. All have a conspicuous dark mask extending from the nostrils to the shoulders, and round, sticky toe pads.

Washington has four native species of true frogs. Red-legged frogs are found throughout western Washington from sea level to about 2,800 feet. They are brown with black spots, and the inside of the hind legs is red. During breeding season they occupy a variety of freshwater wetlands, but they are most frequently encountered near forest streams during the rest of the year.

The Cascades frog looks somewhat similar to the red-legged frog but lacks the red coloring under its legs and is rarely found below 2,000 feet. It is most common in small subalpine pools but also inhabits a wide variety of freshwater wetlands in the mountains. The name is misleading, since it is also found in the Olympics.

The spotted frog is found in parts of the Cascade mountains and in eastern Washington. Until the 1970s it was present in the Puget lowlands, but it has apparently been eliminated by habitat reduction and predation by bullfrogs and imported fish species. The spotted frog is brown or green with fuzzy black spots and has orange or red-orange on the inside of the hind legs and on the lower belly. It is almost always found in the grassy areas around permanent lakes and ponds.

The northern leopard frog is found in Washington mainly at Potholes Reservoir and along the middle Columbia River and the Snake River. The leopard frog is brown or green with dark spots, each spot with a lighter-colored ring around it. The belly is creamy white. Leopard frogs can be found in wet meadows and along streams where there is an abundance of covering vegetation. In the fall, look for them in the cockleburs near streams. They lay their eggs in the shallow vegetated areas at pond edges.

In the United States, the primitive tailed frog is found only in the Pacific Northwest and is a member of the bell toad family. The "tail" of the male tailed frog is a copulatory device that inseminates the female. The male grasps the female just above the hind legs during copulation. A suckerlike mouth structure allows the tadpole to hold on to rocks and other stationary objects in fast-running mountain streams. Tailed frogs occur from sea level to timberline. Their preferred habitat is near permanent, fast-moving streams surrounded by deep forest, common only in montane settings. Active primarily during periods of high relative humidity, the frogs hide under rocks and logs during the day and emerge at night to feed. Tailed frogs do not say much when they are out of water, although they may vocalize underwater. These frogs disappear from streams that pass through logged areas where excessive siltation muddies the water and temperatures climb with full exposure to the sun.

We have two introduced frog species. The bullfrog is by far the more common and more destructive. Found throughout the state at elevations below 1,100 feet, it is most common in western Washington. Bullfrogs are large and pale to dark green with dark spots. The belly is light with dark marbling. Bullfrogs rarely range far from the vegetated edges of permanent ponds, lakes, or sloughs. They are rapacious and eat anything they can catch and swallow. Their diet includes insects, fish, other amphibians, small mammals, and birds. If you hear a loud chirp followed by a plop as you walk near a wet border, you have probably startled a young bullfrog. Bullfrogs outcompete other species because their tadpoles are not eaten as often as other frogs' tadpoles.

The other introduced frog is the green frog, which is known to occur in Lake Washington, in Seattle; in Toad Lake, near Bellingham; and in Lake Gillette, in northeastern Washington. The green frog looks much like the bullfrog but has a prominent fold extending back from each eye. It feeds primarily on aquatic insects.

We have three native species of toads, distinguished from frogs primarily by their dry, warty skin and relatively short hind legs. The western toad is found in all regions of Washington except the driest parts of the Columbia Basin. Body color varies, but there is always a thin white stripe down the middle of the back. Western toads are common near marshes but are rarely seen outside of breeding season, since they are nocturnal. The tadpoles are gregarious and form large schools along pond margins. Probably because of habitat loss, the western toad is now fairly uncommon in the Puget lowlands.

The Great Basin spadefoot is found in the Columbia Basin near ponds and irrigation ditches. The eggs develop and hatch very quickly, and the tadpoles may metamorphose within a few weeks. The Great Basin spadefoot may spend as many as 7 or 8 months a year in a dormant state. This toad is gray with light striping and has numerous dark bumps on its skin. The bottom of each hind foot has a conspicuous black spade that aids in digging into the soil.

Least common is the Woodhouse toad, which is found only along the Snake and Columbia rivers in southeastern Washington. It is widely distributed in the rest of the United States.

ARTHROPODS

Arthropods comprise about four-fifths of all known animals. With their skeleton on the outside of their body they must have jointed appendages. As they grow, their skeleton is shed. Arthropods include the crustaceans, the spiders, and the insects. Crustaceans such as shrimp and crabs are familiar to us, but many are tiny, can be seen only with magnification, and constitute a significant part of marine and freshwater food chains. One important role they play is as decomposers.

Crustaceans: Crustaceans include the ostracods, or seed shrimps, which have their bodies enclosed in a tiny bivalve shell that looks like that of a clam. Less than a tenth of an inch long, they are scavengers on bacteria, molds, and algae. Some fish eat them; some tapeworms use them as a host.

Fairy shrimp, 1 inch long, are colorful back-swimmers, often living in small ponds and temporary pools. They feed on detritus, bacteria, and one-celled organisms; the females carry a pouch of eggs behind their legs. Water fleas are compressed from side to side and swim through the water in short jerks by using their antennae. Their waving legs create a current of water that sweeps tinier animals and algae into their mouths. An important link in the food chain, water fleas may reach a concentration of 300 individuals in a quart of water in the summer. Developing eggs can often be seen through the body wall.

Copepods are about a tenth of an inch long and look somewhat like elongated trilobites. Filter feeders, they use mouth bristles to strain tiny planktonic plants and animals out of the water. Species in this group produce both resistant eggs, which can survive being dried out, and eggs that develop quickly. During breeding season, one- or two-egg sacs develop on each female. Large red females are frequently observed in our fresh water.

Most of the isopods are terrestrial, known to us as woodlice and armadillo bugs. They require the high humidity of rotting logs and the edges of ponds. One genus, *Asellus*, is an aquatic and can be found lumbering across plant stems. The females carry their eggs in a pouch on the underside of their abdomen.

Amphipods are flattened from side to side and have trouble walking on land but swim effectively on their sides. They live close to the bottom or cling to submerged plants and avoid the light. Found in ponds and lakes, they are important members of the eelgrass beds. Their food includes living and dead plants and other detritus. They are eaten by a variety of fish, crabs, and migrating birds.

Crustaceans also include the decapods: the shrimp, the crayfish, and the crabs. Freshwater shrimp, known as prawns, are smaller than crayfish, the freshwater equivalent of lobster. All are omnivorous, some as predators and some as scavengers. Many are eaten by wading birds, frogs, raccoons, mink, and turtles. Many provide a home for one-celled animals and algae, which attach themselves and are carried to new sources of food. Some smaller organisms live in a commensal relationship on their gills and gill chambers. Commensal relationships occur when two organisms live together—usually one upon another—and both lives are enhanced by the arrangement. One might receive a steady food supply through its presence on the other organism, while the larger organism might have its gills cleaned or some other task performed for it. The young of all crustaceans, released into the water as free-swimming or floating organisms, provide an important food source for smaller organisms .

Arachnids: Spiders and mites are arachnids, another group of arthropods. They are distinguished by having eight legs. None of our spiders is aquatic, although some go below the surface of the water enveloped in a bubble of air. Most skitter around on the surface film, occasionally catching prey. Bright-red water mites are common in pond water, swimming around or crawling on vegetation. They seldom come to the surface for air. Mites feed on insects and worms and are partial to mosquito larvae; they also prey on ostracods, water-fleas, and copepods. Some of the larvae attach themselves as external parasites to insects and other invertebrates.

Insects: The insects are a huge group of invertebrates, dominant in freshwater environments. Inevitably they live in wetlands, either as larvae or later as adults. The most common insect orders will be treated here.

Mayflies (Ephemeroptera) are primitive insects whose larval stages are an important food source for dragonfly larvae, beetles, and fish. The young, called nymphs, have three tail prongs and numerous gilled flaps on the side of the abdomen. For four years they feed on diatoms and other plant tissues, converting plant cells to animal tissue. The adult males, with huge membranous wings and two long tail filaments, swarm over water waiting for females to hatch. Adult life lasts only a few days, during which eggs are laid but food is not eaten. Birds eat the adults.

Dragonflies and damselflies (*Odonata*) both have two pairs of membranous wings. Dragonflies are larger and, when resting, hold their wings horizontal to their body. Damselflies are smaller and more delicate than the dragons and hold their wings vertically over their body when at rest. The dragonfly adults hunt near water and are fiercely territorial. They will survey their territory from a high point and always return to that same perch. Both catch masses of smaller insects, usually by hunting on the wing. The aquatic nymphs are dominant pond carnivores, feeding on insects, tadpoles, and small fish. Some sit and wait for prey, others stalk. Their power lies in the length of their lower lip, which is hinged, allowing it to drop down, shoot out, grab a worm, and pull it back immediately.

Stoneflies (*Plecoptera*) usually do not feed as adults. They are brownish, inch-long insects with two long antennae and membranous wings folded flat over their back. The nymphs are important fish food in ponds.

Some members of the order Hemiptera live permanently in the water. Most overwinter in the bottom mud as adults and produce a single generation a year. Their mouth parts are piercing and sucking jointed beaks. Included in this group is the huge predatory giant water bug. Up to 2½ inches long with a flat oval brown body, it grabs its prey with its front legs and uses its beak to kill it. It attacks insects, crustaceans, tadpoles, frogs, and fish many times its size. A breathing tube at the end of the abdomen periodically takes in air above the water. The secretive

Dragonfly resting

water scorpions look like brown underwater walking sticks. Slowly back-
ing up a plant stem, they push their abdominally mounted breathing
tube through the water's surface and take in air. Seldom swimming, they
lie in wait for small insects to pass by, then grab them with their
scissorlike front legs.

Backswimmers move underwater with oarlike legs. When resting
they rise to the surface with the tip of their abdomen puncturing the
surface film. As predators, they attack everything they can. Water boatmen have huge eyes, and their middle legs are longer than the rest. The
hind legs are flattened and are used to row the insect along. The fore-
legs are scooplike for sifting out tiny organisms from bottom debris. Fish
eat large quantities of them. Water striders are also in this order. Living
on the surface film, they skate along, using their front legs to grab land

insects that fall onto the surface or any aquatics that come too close to the surface from below.

Coleoptera is a huge order, and many members are aquatic. Beetles have distinctly different stages in their life cycle. With chewing mouthparts and hard wing covers protecting their membranous wings, they are like small tanks. The whirligig beetles, a half-inch long, are continually in motion, twirling about on the water's surface. They have two pairs of eyes, allowing them to see above and below the water simultaneously. They scavenge insects caught in the surface film. Predaceous diving beetles are oval and black and have hind legs flattened and fringed with hairs. They are excellent swimmers, moving their hind legs in unison. Adults feed on any small animals they can grab. Their larvae, called water tigers, have large sicklelike jaws they use to suck their prey's body contents.

Many terrestrial beetles bore for a living, laying eggs in or under bark, with the larvae making winding burrows into the wood of the tree. The willow borer is a dark-colored beetle, around a half-inch long, the male with yellow lines on its face, thorax, and wing covers. The female lays her eggs on willow bark. The minute, reddish yellow willow leaf beetle chews holes in willow leaves and eats the buds. Several species of the genus *Donacia* feed on pond lilies, pickerelweed, and other wetland plants. After cutting a hole in the lily pad, the female cements her eggs to the bottom surface of the leaves with her abdomen. The larvae spin a shelter beneath the leaf, and 10 months later an adult emerges.

As larvae, caddis flies (Tricoptera) are ingenious case builders. All aquatic, the larvae use parts of sticks or sand grains or small stones to build funnel-shaped cases, which they drag along the bottom of streams. Omnivorous, the case makers eat small crustaceans, insects, worms, diatoms, and plant parts by feeding from the front of the tube. Adults are 1½ inches long and mothlike, with brown papery wings folded like a fan and long back-curved antennae. They are a significant part of the diet of trout and other fish.

The true flies (Diptera) have a single pair of wings, the second pair having been modified into tiny gyroscopes. Large compound eyes, piercing or sucking mouth parts, and great variation mark this order. The midges, often mistaken for mosquitoes, are commonly found near water. Most adults do not bite. The *Chironomus* larvae, called bloodworms, are red. An oxygen-bearing pigment chemically related to the hemoglobin of human blood gives the entire worm a bright red color.

This molecule allows it to survive in low oxygen levels. The larvae are important fish food.

Only female mosquitoes take blood meals, necessary for egg development. The larvae, called wrigglers, may be a half-inch long. A set of brushes around the mouth filters out microscopic organic debris. They rest at the surface but snap to the bottom when disturbed. Adults are eaten by birds and bats, and the larvae are important fish and insect food. Crane flies look like giant mosquitoes, although they are larger insects, often reaching 2 to 3 inches. Their legs are long and delicate and often lose segments. The aquatic larvae, called leather jackets, live in mats of algae. The adults may be vegetarian or predaceous or eat nothing.

Hover flies, mimicking bees with their yellow and black stripes, have aquatic larvae called rat-tailed maggots. They live in bottom debris in shallow water and breathe through a 1-inch tube that extends above the water's surface. Horsefly and deerfly larvae are aquatic. The eggs fall into the water from overhanging vegetation and develop in the mud. Adult females bite, but males live on nectar.

Many butterflies and moths (*Lepidoptera*) take advantage of the food, shelter, and moisture found in wetlands. Those wetlands with the most sun and the greatest variety of flowers as nectar sources attract the most butterflies. The Lepidoptera have mouthparts modified into coils, an adaptation for sucking nectar out of flowers. Their two pairs of wings are shingled with overlapping scales. Few are aquatic, although the adult of one genus of moth lays its eggs on the underside of floating leaves. After hatching, the larva sews together pieces of the leaf, making a protective case that it drags around with it as it feeds.

One could expect to find the following butterflies and moths feeding or traveling through wetlands: the western tiger swallowtail, viceroy, tortoiseshell, arctic skipper, Freya's fritillary, northern blue, and common alpine butterflies and the Cerisy's sphinx and jutta arctic moths.

BIRDS

With all of the excellent bird field guides currently available, we will not repeat species descriptions. Instead, we offer an abbreviated list of the more common wetland bird species. An outstanding daily report on the presence of birds in Washington can be found on the Internet on the listserve Tweeters (See Further Reading section).

The various national wildlife refuges are good places to begin wetland bird-watching. Many of the refuges were established to protect or restore wetlands used by migratory birds or to provide habitat for endangered species. Most of the refuges offer bird lists indicating seasonal species sighted at the refuge. It is a good idea to call ahead for information, as migratory birds don't always travel by our calendar. Birds described here are listed in their apparent order of evolution, loons being the most primitive and ancient order and various perching birds, such as finches and sparrows, the most recently evolved.

Loons: From fall through spring all five existing species of loon can be found in western Washington, almost exclusively on marine waters. All of them breed and nest on northern lakes, but individual birds may be seen here during the summer months. Loons are sleek birds best known for their haunting call during breeding months. Males and females look identical and molt twice a year, having a dull winter plumage and a distinctive summer breeding plumage.

The red-throated loon, Pacific loon, common loon, and yellow-billed loon are all seen readily in the San Juan Islands; the red-throated and common loon are found at the Nisqually Delta during all except the summer months and at Dungeness in the winter. The arctic and common loons are seen in Willapa Bay during the winter and spring.

Grebes: Grebes are similar to loons in having their legs placed far to the rear of their bodies and in preferring to escape enemies by diving rather than flying. Male and female grebes are indistinguishable year-round. Grebes do not have webbed feet but have lobed toes with partial webbing.

Only the pied-billed grebe nests here, spending most of the year on quiet ponds and lakes, although occasionally it can be seen on salt water during migration or when a cold snap has frozen its usual freshwater home. The horned and red-necked grebe overwinter along the coast, and the eared grebe prefers Turnbull but heads for the coast when it gets really cold.

Pelicans: The American white pelican is a spectacular bird with a wingspan of about 9 feet, a huge orange bill, and dazzling black-and-white plumage. A bird of inland lakes, it can be found with some regularity in the Gloyd Seeps and Potholes areas. The white pelican does not dive for its prey but paddles and flaps around in the shallows, often in groups, pushing the fish toward the shore, where they can be easily scooped up. Initially, white pelican young are featherless and extremely susceptible to heat prostration. The adults shield them from the sun, but many chicks are lost because of human disturbance to the nesting colonies. Other threats are insecticide poisoning and hunters, who may confuse the pelican with the snow goose.

Cormorants: Two species of cormorant, Brandt's and the pelagic, are strictly marine and can be seen year-round at Dungeness, at Willapa Bay, and in the San Juans. Another species, the double-crested, builds a nest of sticks in trees or on rocky cliffs near deep inland lakes or on the coast. Nisqually hosts the double-crested cormorant year-round, although it doesn't nest there. These dark goose-sized birds are familiar to everyone who has ridden a ferry, since they are often seen perched on pilings, spreading their wings to dry.

Bitterns and Herons: The American bittern resides in many of our freshwater marshes, usually nesting in heavily reeded areas or among cattails. Although represented statewide, it is uncommon. It has a distinctive pumping call in the spring and early summer.

The great blue heron, 4 feet tall and armed with a long, sharp bill and a raucous voice, is the most often seen and identified heron in the state. It is found year-round in both salt and freshwater marshes, usually hunting alone. Nesting is in large, noisy rookeries, with many nests found in the same tree. The great blue heron eats anything it can catch—fish, frogs, mice, snakes, turtles—and is a real pest at some fish hatcheries and backyard ponds.

The green heron, or green-backed heron, is relatively uncommon in the Pacific Northwest but can be found in freshwater marshes and sloughs in western Washington. It nests at the Nisqually Delta. The great egret, a snow white bird slightly smaller than the great blue heron, has been seen occasionally in southwestern Washington and even more rarely in the summer months in eastern Washington marshes. Black-crested heron are common in the ponds and marshes of eastern Washington, especially in the Potholes area.

Swans: All native swans, the largest of our waterfowl, are fully protected by law. One species, the trumpeter swan, was hunted almost to extinction, with fewer than a hundred birds counted in 1931. Wintering populations are seen with some frequency from the Columbia River to the San Juan Islands.

The slightly smaller tundra swan is more common and can be found overwintering in freshwater marshes and ponds in western Washington. Migration to the nesting grounds in northern Alaska and Canada begins in March; this is the time of year when large concentrations of tundra swans can be found in eastern Washington ponds.

The mute swan is a European export that is found most widely in parks, but some have naturalized. The mute can be easily distinguished from the other swan species on the basis of its large, knobbed bill. Orcas Island has a documented breeding site for mute swans.

Geese: The Canada goose is the best known and most easily recognized. Its distinctive honking call and white cheek patch on black head are positive identifying characteristics. The Canada goose nests in both eastern and western Washington and overwinters at places like McNary, Turnbull, and Nisqually.

The single largest winter population of the brant is found on Padilla Bay, where the eelgrass and sea lettuce that are its chief food occur. The brant nests on the northern coastal tundra of Alaska and Canada. Although it is hunted extensively, the greatest danger to this species lies in habitat loss.

The white snow goose is sometimes mistaken for a swan, but the smaller body, shorter neck, and black wing tips are the distinctive identifying characteristics. Snow geese breed in Siberia and arctic Canada. Most overwinter in the California Central Valley, but a significant population spends the winter moving between the Skagit and Fraser River deltas.

Black brant

Ducks: Defining lifestyles is one way to sort through the ducks. Perching ducks are represented by the wood duck. Threatened with extinction early in the century as a result of habitat destruction and overhunting, the wood duck is making a comeback in wildlife refuges. Wood ducks are seen most often around the edges of small ponds and slow-moving flows in areas with nesting sites. The young ducklings leap from their nest cavity high up in trees and stumps only minutes after hatching.

The dabbling ducks forage by tipping up and stretching to reach for food, rather than by diving beneath the surface. They prefer shallow water and are found on freshwater ponds and marshes. All of the dabbling ducks, such as the mallards, have a bright, iridescent wing patch. Other species are the teals (green-winged, blue-winged, and cinnamon), northern pintails, northern shovelers, gadwalls, and wigeons. These duck species can be found throughout the state most of the year.

Diving ducks include the redhead, common along the lower Columbia River and at Turnbull. Other diving ducks are the canvasback, nesting in eastern Washington and wintering on eelgrass beds along the coast. This group also includes the ring-necked duck, a common migrant but rare nester, and the scaups. The greater scaup prefers marine habitats and is most likely to be seen along the coast, while the lesser scaup prefers fresh water and is commonly found nesting along inland waters.

Sea ducks are the best divers and, as the name implies, most likely to be found near the coast. The harlequin duck, oldsquaw, scoters, goldeneyes, and bufflehead are all seen with varying degrees of abundance in the winter months at Dungeness, at Nisqually, in Willapa Bay, and in the San Juans. Most are tundra nesters, but nonbreeding individuals can be seen year-round.

The mergansers are crested ducks with long, pointed bills adapted for handling fish. Hooded mergansers prefer fresh water and often associate with wood ducks. They nest in tree cavities or nesting boxes but tend to be found around faster-moving water than wood ducks. The hooded merganser is a year-round resident and can be seen from the Columbia River north to British Columbia. Common mergansers prefer larger open bodies of fresh water but may be found floating in rafts and fishing for herring along the coast. A few common mergansers may nest locally. The red-breasted merganser is a common migrant and winter visitor, most likely to be found on the estuaries of northern Puget Sound, on the Dungeness Spit, and in the San Juan Islands.

Our sole representative of the stiff-tailed ducks is the ruddy duck. Seen in its summer plumage, the male has a bright chestnut brown body and an electric blue bill. Ruddy ducks spend most of the year on deep freshwater ponds or lakes bordered by cattails and bulrushes. They are excellent divers and prefer to escape danger by diving rather than flying. Ruddy ducks are particularly common at Turnbull Wildlife Refuge, leaving for the coast only in the coldest months of winter.

Eagles, Hawks, and Falcons: The osprey, a large fish-eating hawk, builds a bulky nest made of sticks and placed high near water. The osprey feeds exclusively on fish, plunging feetfirst into the water to grasp its prey. Nesting sites are scattered through the state near good fishing holes. Occasional individuals winter here, but most migrate south in early winter and return very early in the spring.

The bald eagle is a prime birding attraction in the San Juan Islands and at the Skagit Delta. About 60 pairs of eagles nest in the San Juans, but during the winter more than 250 individuals are present. In the fall, population numbers drop; this is the time to check the Skagit River, since the eagles are following the salmon runs and feeding on dead or dying spawned fish. Eagles mate for life and have long life spans but are extremely sensitive to human disturbances and so have difficulty finding or maintaining nesting sites.

Northern harriers, or marsh hawks, swoop over freshwater and saltwater marshes throughout the state. They are specialized mousers but will also take small waterfowl and shorebirds should the opportunity arise.

Other birds of prey commonly seen near wetlands are the red-tailed hawk, found statewide as it hunts for small mammals in open areas; the merlin, a small falcon that is a fairly common migrant and winter visitor; the American kestrel, a tiny, swift raptor that prefers insects in the summer months; and the peregrine falcon. The peregrine is the fastest bird in the world, reaching almost 200 miles per hour in attack dives, and it is large enough to take ducks and other medium-sized waterfowl.

Rails and Coots: The Virginia rail and the sora are common in freshwater marshes of Washington. Both are shy, elusive birds probably best known for their distinctive calls. Both nest here; some are year-round residents, but most individuals migrate south in the fall. Both have compressed, narrow bodies that can slip quickly through dense wetland vegetation, and long toes that prevent them from sinking into the muck.

Often seen in the company of ducks, the American coot, or marsh hen, is gregarious. A novice birder may well mistake the coot, with its rounded dark body, its large pale bill, and its dabbling, for a duck. They do not have webbed feet but instead have long-toed, lobed feet. They inhabit freshwater ponds and marshes throughout the state, leaving for shallow saltwater sites only when their home ponds freeze over.

Cranes: One place to reliably see the sandhill crane is at the Ridgefield Wildlife Refuge, where a fairly large population spends the winter feeding in the marshes and on the corn and grain grown at the refuge. The last half of April and September at Potholes is also a good opportunity. The sandhill crane flies with both neck and feet outstretched, usually calling in a loud, musical voice.

Shorebirds: This is a large and diverse group of birds that feed at the water's edge along the coast of Washington. Some sixty species of shorebirds either live here or pass through on annual migrations. Sandy shores and estuaries are attractive destinations.

Identifying the many species of shorebirds can be complex; to the novice, one sandpiper looks pretty much like every other sandpiper, and identification is made more difficult because shorebird plumage, often only subtly different from one species to the next, varies seasonally and with age. Shape of the bill, feeding style, flight style, overall shape, size, and coloration are all important characteristics.

The killdeer is the most common plover to nest here. This bird tries to lure the intruder away with its call and its broken-wing trick. The snowy plover nests at the Leadbetter Unit of the Willapa Bay Wildlife Refuge; the area is closed during nesting season.

Black oystercatchers nest regularly in the San Juans, less often elsewhere in Washington. They are nonmigratory and can be seen on the rocky beaches all winter long, feeding on limpets and other mollusks.

The stilts and avocets breed on our interior marshes, although Washington is at the northern edge of their distribution. Occasional migratory stragglers may be seen on the coast as they pass to and from their wintering grounds in South America.

More than thirty sandpiper species visit our shorelines regularly; most are seen during migration. Willapa Bay and Grays Harbor, at peak migration in April and May, are the places to go to practice sandpiper identification. Dunlins and sanderlings winter here regularly. Most species nest in the Arctic and migrate south to the tropics. The distances these birds fly underscores the extreme importance of staging areas such as Willapa Bay and Grays Harbor, where the birds can stop and replenish body fat stores for the next flight leg, which may be as much as 1,500 miles.

Gulls and Terns: The gulls are familiar and well-known birds of the Northwest, although few people take the trouble to differentiate between the ten or so different species present. Two species, the ring-billed gull and the California gull, nest in eastern Washington. McNary Wildlife Refuge, near Pasco, is an excellent place to watch for them.

The glaucous-winged gulls are breeding here, and there are several large gulleries in the San Juan Islands. Bonaparte's gull, much smaller and with a black head in summer, is a common migrant in Puget Sound and the San Juans.

Terns are graceful, gull-like birds, smaller than most gulls and having, at least in the summer, black caps. Terns feed by diving headfirst into the water after fish. The common and Caspian's tern are seen along the coast during spring and fall migrations; Forster's tern spends its summers in the Great Basin marshes nests near the Potholes reservoir. The black tern is a common nesting bird at Turnbull.

Owls: Rarely seen because of nocturnal habits but often heard, owls are an important part of any food web. They consume huge quantities of rodents. The great horned owl will take anything smaller than itself. None of the owls is specifically a wetland bird, but wetlands and surrounding grassy areas are rich feeding grounds. The great horned owl is most common on the east side of the Cascades, the short-eared owl more common on the west side. When lemming populations dip in the Arctic, snowy owls travel south in winter and may be seen on the Olympic Peninsula and at the Skagit Delta.

Kingfishers: The belted kingfisher is a familiar sight, and its incessant call is a familiar sound along almost any body of water. Other than the common Steller's jay, the kingfisher is the only crested blue bird in the area. It is a permanent resident.

Woodpeckers: The downy woodpecker is the most likely to be seen in a wetland, since it favors deciduous trees and is often found in cottonwoods and willows.

Flycatchers: Aggressive hunters of winged insects, flycatchers are often overlooked and can be difficult to identify. The eastern kingbird nests along ponds or streams, especially at Turnbull. The willow flycatcher can be found in brushy areas along streams and nests on both sides of the Cascades. With a preference for moist, wooded habitats, the western flycatcher is most common west of the Cascades.

Swallows: Tree swallows are the first to reappear in the spring. They prefer wet habitats with plenty of old snags. The barn swallow is most likely to nest away from wetlands, but since swallows are insect feeders, wetlands provide food. With the exception of the bank swallow, which nests mainly in eastern Washington, swallows of all species can be found in abundance throughout the state.

Miscellaneous Perching Birds: The brown creeper feeds on bark insects and is a common inhabitant of forested swamps. Marsh wrens breed in the marshes and wet meadows of both eastern and western Washington. Visually inconspicuous, they are highly territorial and extremely vocal. Each male builds several nests, hoping to entice a female to one of them; the rest are left vacant. A few wrens are year-round residents, occasionally extending their range into salt marshes during the colder months.

The water pipit nests in the mountains above timberline and feeds on insects at the edges of alpine ponds or on insects frozen in snowbanks. Pipits winter on the coast and are found in treeless areas, such as sandy shores or mown fields or along marsh edges.

The yellow warbler nests in moist thickets and along the edges of bogs throughout the state. It is a favorite target of the cowbird, which lays one egg in the warbler's nest. The cowbird chick hatches early and crowds out the legitimate warbler young. If a yellow warbler female discovers an alien egg, she covers the entire clutch with a new nesting layer and starts again. Yellow warblers nesting near cattail-rush ponds enjoy some freedom from the cowbird, as red-winged blackbirds vigilantly repel these intruders.

The common yellowthroat female is rarely seen, but the male often climbs high to deliver his characteristic mating call. The common yellowthroat is widespread in marshes and in stream thickets from coast to coast.

Red-winged blackbirds are one of our best-recognized wetland birds. The males are highly territorial and sing vigorously to announce their presence. They chase intruders of any size from the nesting area but in the fall revert to friendly, flocking behavior. Yellow-headed blackbirds are conspicuous in the marshes of eastern Washington during the spring, summer, and early fall, but most migrate south for the winter. They maximize good nesting grounds by crowding together as closely as twenty-five nests in 15 square feet.

Lincoln's sparrow lives in mountain bogs and wet meadows. It nests in the northern boreal forest and in the mountains south to California. A common migrant along the coast, its peak fall migration is in September.

FISH

Unique to the western Olympic Peninsula and the state of Washington, the Olympic mudminnow prefers heavy vegetation in still backwaters. A small fish, less than 2½ inches long, it is light brown with spotty stripes. This fish is unique to the state and deserves protection.

The minnow family is important as food for larger fish. The carp is the largest of the minnows, sometimes reaching fifty pounds. Inhabiting warm shallow fresh water, it is tolerant of pollution, low oxygen, and extreme variations of temperature. Carp move into warm, weedy shallows in late spring to spawn.

During the warm summer months it is possible to see large schools of redside shiners in the shallow areas of lakes and streams, usually residing in dense vegetation. Found in all the Pacific Coast states, this species is quite common in Washington. Its distinguishing characteristics are the oblique angle to its mouth and its compressed body. The redside shiner is forage for many other species. At times shiners make up as much as 90 percent of a trout's diet; however, they do compete with small trout for insects and snails.

Members of the catfish family can survive in low-oxygen water and may burrow into the mud and hibernate. The most common bullhead in the Northwest, the brown bullhead lives in warm-water lakes, ponds, and streams. All bullheads make saucer-shaped nests in April to June. When hatched the fry are herded around in the shallows by the parents until the end of summer, when they move back into the deeper portions of the lake or stream. They are omnivorous feeders and are sometimes destructive to fish eggs and young fish.

The three-spined stickleback is found in freshwater and saltwater habitats nearly all over the world. In the Northwest it is common in most of the lakes and streams and some stream mouths. It prefers to live close to the bottom in or around vegetation in the marshy areas of lakes and streams. Stickleback can be identified by the three large spines in the dorsal fin, and they average about 1½ inches long. Their sides have no scales but rather a series of bony plates. The number of bony plates is related to exposure to predation. The male stickleback builds a nest on the bottom of the marsh and then does an elaborate dance to entice the female to lay her eggs in it. After successfully mating, the male will guard the nest until the young hatch and disperse. During this time the males will attack anything that comes within range of the nest, even scuba divers.

While not a native of the Pacific Northwest, the largemouth bass can be found in most of the lowland lakes and many of the warmer river systems. The largemouth has eliminated native trout populations from many lakes. It prefers the weedy shallow backwaters of lakes and streams, often lying in water barely deep enough to cover its back. In extremely hot or cold weather the bass moves to deeper water. The largemouth will eat nearly anything; small fish are the primary items of its diet.

The black crappie can be found throughout the Northwest. Black crappie prefer northern water and dense vegetation over sand when the water is cool. When the water warms up in the summer, the fish move into the cooler deep water. Crappie move into shallow, weedy water to spawn in the early spring; adults afterwards school in the adjoining waters.

White crappie occupy the same general range as the black crappie with the white more prevalent in the southern parts of the state. White crappie also are able to handle turbid or alkaline water somewhat better than the black. Both black and white crappie enjoy spawning in brush piles and areas with a lot of vegetation on which to deposit the egg masses. The female builds a 5- to 6-inch nest of algae on the vegetation, which is guarded by the male until the fry hatch and disperse.

Bluegill, an introduced species, prefers ponds with weeded areas. Like most sunfishes it is tolerant of high water temperatures but is intolerant of low oxygen levels and is among the first to die in a winterkill lake. (Winterkill happens when ice and snow cut off the sunlight reaching the pond, thereby stopping any photosynthesis and oxygen production. Respiration continues, however, and carbon dioxide builds up in the pond.) The fish's popularity has led to its being introduced into many small ponds and lakes, where the population quickly outgrows the food supply, stunting the fish. In lakes with a large group of predators (bass, walleye, or fishermen) the bluegills do very well.

The pumpkinseed, also known as sunfish, prefers calm, clear water with thick vegetation and somewhat cooler temperatures than the bluegill. Pumpkinseed are very territorial and will often chase larger fish out of their bounded areas. The mouth is very small, but strong teeth in the throat allow the fish to consume mollusks and crustaceans. These fish often spawn several times a year using a nest built by the male. Guarded by the male, the nests can produce up to 8,000 fry. The nests resemble those of the bluegill and the warmouth. Hybridization with these species is common.

Yellow perch is one of the most common fish found in the lowland lakes and streams of the Northwest. In the spring the perch move into the shallow wetlands bordering the lakes to spawn. They may stay in the shallows for several months. As the water warms up in the summer they move back into the deeper areas of the lake. These fish school in groups of like size and age and stay in the same general area for most of their adult life. Yellow perch are very prolific and will overpopulate a lake or pond if not controlled through predation or fishing.

There are five species of native salmon in the Pacific Northwest—chum, pink, coho, chinook, and sockeye—and two species of native trout: rainbow and cutthroat. Sea-run rainbow are called steelhead. The Dolly Varden is our only native char; brook and lake trout are introduced char species.

All of the salmonids are characterized by long, streamlined bodies, round scales, and a fatty dorsal fin. All of the salmonids spend the greater part of their lives either in the ocean or in cold, deep, or fast-moving fresh water and, in general, have little contact with wetlands as described here. However, juvenile salmon often congregate in estuaries and feed on zooplankton before entering the ocean. Trout fry feed on the larval and aquatic insects that are so numerous in the marshy fringes of lakes.

MAMMALS

Bats: Bats are the only true flying mammals, whereas other "fliers," such as the flying squirrel, are gliders. Most bats navigate and locate food by sonar. A high-pitched sound is produced by the larynx, and the bat listens for an echo to bounce back from its prey. In less than a second, a bat can locate its prey, sweep it up with its wing, pop it into its mouth, and continue on the hunt. Many species are now endangered because of habitat loss, human disturbances during hibernation, and loss or pollution of insect food sources because of pesticide use in agriculture.

The little brown bat, *Myotis lucifugus*, is one of the most common bat species in North America. It weighs about a quarter-ounce and is from 3 to 4 inches long. It leaves its roost at dusk to hunt insects. It seems to prefer mosquitoes, but its diet includes mayflies, flies, moths, and beetles. Members of the genus *Myotis* are widely distributed, living in every region except the Arctic.

Beaver: The largest rodent in North America, the beaver is superbly adapted for a wetland life. It spends almost half its day swimming and the rest of its time and energy building dams across streams to create ponds. On land, beaver are awkward and slow. The pond is their security, and if food sources run short near the pond, the dam is built higher to raise the water level and bring water and food closer together.

The beaver can swim up to 5 miles per hour and can remain submerged for up to 15 minutes. Underwater, it closes off its ears and nostrils with valves, skin flaps seal off the mouth, and clear membranes cover the eyes. Secretions of castoreum, applied by hind feet equipped with special nails that serve as combs, waterproof the fur. Beaver apparently mate for life. Kits, usually four or five in a litter, are born in late spring or early summer. They can swim by the time they are a week old.

Mink: This short-tempered, voracious carnivore lives alone along rivers, creeks, lakes, marshes, and ponds, where it can find its favorite prey, the muskrat. Rabbits, mice, birds, fish, snakes, frogs, even turtles are all taken by the ever-hungry mink. Although seemingly the ultimate carnivore, the mink is not the top of the food chain; it is preyed upon by the larger owls, bobcats, coyotes, and, of course, humans.

The mink has a long (19- to 28-inch), sleek body and a long, slightly bushy tail. The lustrous brown-to-black fur has long been used to make coats and stoles, although most of the demand for pelts is now met by commercial mink farmers. Distribution is from the Arctic to Florida in all except very dry areas.

Mountain Beaver: Not a beaver and not confined to the mountains, the mountain beaver is found most commonly in tangled thickets of salmonberry and thimbleberry along streams and wet meadows. This primitive rodent is the last of a group that goes back to the Eocene, 50 million years ago. The mountain beaver does not breed until it is almost two years old, and it has small litters of only two to three kits. Growing to 18 inches long with tiny ears and eyes and a very short tail, they have dark brown fur. Pacific Northwest Indians once used the pelts to make robes. The burrows are large and surrounded by mounds of earth. In late summer, the vegetarian mountain beaver cures mounds of "hay" near the mouth of its burrow. When living near urban areas, mountain beaver are often a puzzlement to gardeners when they harvest stalks of prize flowers and haul them away for hay.

Muskrat: Muskrat thrive in freshwater marshes and along streams over most of North America. Named for its ratlike appearance and musky odor, the muskrat is more closely related to mice than rats. It has a dense, glossy brown fur coat and has been trapped extensively for 200 years. Even now, about 10 million are taken annually. Fortunately for the species, they reach sexual maturity at 6 weeks and may have two to eight litters per year. Muskrats fall prey to mink, snapping turtles, foxes, raccoon, otters, bobcats, hawks, and owls, in addition to man. Weighing in at 3 pounds and 16 to 25 inches long, the muskrat will fight and can hold its own against larger animals. It is most vulnerable when caught away from the water and its burrow.

Muskrat build domed lodges using aquatic plants, especially cattails. They also build feeding platforms or rafts, where they dine on roots and shoots, crayfish, frogs, fish, and freshwater clams. Although present in Washington, they do not reach the concentrations found in the Midwest; consequently, they have a much-reduced impact here.

Nutria: An introduced species from South America, the nutria, or coypu, is most common and successful along the Gulf Coast, but it also does well in the Pacific Northwest. Busy burrowers and tunnelers, nutria can cause extensive damage to dikes and streambanks. They are also insatiable eaters, feeding on cattails, sedges, and other waterweeds.

Nutria are large rodents about 3 feet long weighing 8 to 20 pounds. They have long, hairless tails. The thick fur has been in demand for fur coats and was the reason for bringing the species to North America. Inevitably, they escaped. The young can be seen triumphantly riding on the swimming female's back, periodically leaning down for a quick mouthful of milk from the highly placed mammary glands.

Raccoon: This masked, ring-tailed mammal is familiar to most Northwest dwellers. Although not aquatic, the raccoon can and does swim and prefers to live near wetlands. It is an opportunistic feeder, happy with corn from fields, crayfish and frogs from streams and ponds, or Twinkies from suburban picnics.

Raccoons have dexterous front feet that function as nervous, sensitive hands. No nook or cranny is left unexplored in the raccoon's nocturnal search for food. Sprightly and intelligent, raccoons are among the most playful of animals, and their penchant for marshmallows often becomes an obsession.

Shrew: Shrews are widely distributed in North America, ranging from deserts to rain forests and from sea level to mountains. Of particular interest here is the water shrew, usually found in wet, boggy areas near forest streams. Although water shrews can swim, they rarely plunge in, preferring to forage for insects, worms, spiders, and small mollusks along the banks. Water shrews have hairy toes on their back feet; the hair traps air bubbles and allows the shrew to actually run on the surface of the water for short distances.

Shrews look like mice with long, pointy snouts and are among our most common animals. Water shrews measure up to 6 inches long, half of that length being tail. Females have up to three litters a year, with four to eight young born, but with only six teats, the mother probably raises a maximum of six babies.

Shrew Mole: This is a tiny mammal, less than 5 inches long, that might be mistaken for a shrew because of its long, shrewlike nose. It has dark fur, a short, scaly tail, and the characteristic broadened forefeet. Unique to the Pacific Northwest, it is common but rarely seen. Shrew moles live in damp lowland forests, although along streams their range extends up to higher elevations. They hunt day and night in runways under the surface litter and eat spiders, earthworms, and insects.

Vole: The water vole, also known as Richardson's vole, is found in mountainous areas near streams and lakes. It is a good swimmer and often jumps into the water to escape predators. In summer it burrows near sedges and under willows; in winter it moves away from the water and builds nests under the snow. It eats leafy plants, including valerian, willow buds, lousewort, and lupine. The water vole is one of the larger voles, growing up to 10 inches long and weighing 2 to 3½ ounces. The short, thick fur is gray to brown. Little is known about the water vole's reproduction, but it is believed to have a litter size of three to five young.

Western Harvest Mouse: This small mouse is common in the marshes and wet meadows of eastern Washington. About 6 inches long, this mouse is brown above and whitish underneath. It is a nocturnal feeder and spends the day in a tiny nest made of dry grass. Several litters of four to six young are produced yearly.

Sundew on a floating log at Lake Kapowsin

FURTHER READING

Becker, C. Dale, and Duane Neitzel, eds. *Water Quality in North American River Systems.* Columbus & Richland: Batelle Press, 1992.

Borrer, Donald, and Richard White. *A Field Guide to the Insects.* Boston: Houghton Mifflin Co., 1970.

Conservation Foundation. *Protecting America's Wetlands: An Action Agenda.* Final report of the national wetlands policy forum. Washington, D.C.: Conservation Foundation, 1988.

Dalton, Stephen. *At the Water's Edge: The Secret Life of Lake and Stream.* New York: Portland House Books, 1991.

Ehrlich, Paul, David Dobkin, and Darryl Wheye. *The Birder's Handbook: A Field Guide to the Natural History of North American Birds.* New York: Simon & Schuster, 1988.

Kritzman, Ellen. *Little Mammals of the Pacific Northwest.* Seattle: Pacific Search Press, 1977.

Kruckeberg, Arthur. *The Natural History of Puget Sound Country.* Seattle: University of Washington Press, 1991.

Lean, Geoffrey, and Don Hinrichsen. *World Wildlife Fund Atlas of the Environment.* 2nd ed. New York: HarperPerennial, 1992.

Leonard, William, H. Brown, L. Jones, K. McAllister, R. Storm. *Amphibians of Washington and Oregon.* Seattle: Seattle Audubon Society, 1993.

Michaud, Joy. *At Home with Wetlands: A Landowner's Guide.* Publication 90-31. Olympia: Washington State Department of Ecology, 1990.

Niering, William A. *Wetlands.* Audubon Society Nature Guides. New York: Knopf, 1985.

Nussbaum, Ronald A., E. Brodie, and R. Storm. *Amphibians and Reptiles of the Pacific Northwest.* Moscow: University of Idaho Press, 1983.

Pojar, Jim, and Andy Mackinnon. *Plants of the Pacific Northwest Coast: Washington, Oregon, British Columbia, and Alaska.* Redmond, Wash.: Lone Pine, 1994.

Puget Sound Water Quality Authority. *State of the Sound 1988 Report.* Puget Sound Water Quality Authority, 1988.

Pyle, Robert M. *Watching Washington Butterflies.* Seattle: Seattle Audubon Society, 1974.

Schultz, Stewart T. *The Northwest Coast: A Natural History.* Portland: Timber Press, 1990.

Snively, Gloria. *Exploring the Seashore in British Coumbia, Washington, and Oregon.* Vancouver, B.C.: Gordon Soules, 1978.

Stokes, Donald W. *A Guide to Observing Insect Lives.* Boston: Little, Brown & Co., 1983.

Wahl, Terence, and Dennis Paulson. *A Guide to Bird Finding in Washington.* Bellingham, Wash.: T. R. Wahl, 1991.

Washington State Department of Ecology. *Wetland Regulations Guidebook.* Publication 88-5. Olympia: Washington State Department of Ecology, 1988.

Washington State Department of Ecology. *Wetlands Preservation: An Information and Action Guide.* Publication 90-5. Olympia: Washington State Department of Ecology, 1991.

Wetlands Section, Washington State Department of Ecology. *Washington State Hydric Soils Guidebook.* Publication 90-20. Olympia: Washington State Department of Ecology, 1990.

Wolf, Edward C. *A Tidewater Place: Portrait of the Willapa Ecosystem.* Long Beach, Wash.: Willapa Alliance, 1993.

For Internet users, there is a listserve for information on Washington birds and natural history called Tweeters. To subscribe send a message—sub tweeters *your name*—to listproc@lists.u.washington.edu. Also available on-line is the GreenDisk Paperless Environmental Journal. Address: greendisk@igc.apc.org

INDEX

ABOUT THE AUTHORS

Originally from Bellingham, Washington, MARIE CHURNEY has had a long involvement with conservation issues and environmental education. Currently a professor of science education at Pacific Lutheran University in Tacoma, she has been a teacher for 35 years, working with students from elementary through university levels. She has participated in national committees on environmental education and science education and for several years was the director of an environmental study area in North Carolina. She was extensively involved in the development of the Snake Lake Nature Center, a wetland project in Tacoma, as well as with Northwest Trek and the Point Defiance Zoo. Her spare-time activities include botanizing, kayaking, and making sculpture.

A former student of Dr. Churney's, SUSAN WILLIAMS grew up hiking and fishing in the Pacific Northwest and in college became interested in plant ecology. She currently teaches in a Montessori school. Her hobbies are hiking, reading, writing, and gardening.

OTHER TITLES YOU MAY ENJOY FROM THE MOUNTAINEERS:

Preserving Washington's Wildlands: A Guide to The Nature Conservancy's Preserves in Washington,
The Nature Conservancy of Washington
Color photographs and text profile protected preserves and natural areas.

Washington's Wild Rivers: The Unfinished Work,
Tim McNulty & Pat O'Hara
Prose and full-color photographs explain Northwest rivers, and existing systems for protecting them.

The Enduring Forests: Northern California, Oregon, Washington, British Columbia, and Southeast Alaska,
Ruth Kirk, Editor; Charles Mauzy, Photo Editor
Five regional authors, supported by a remarkable collection of photographs, offer their unique perspectives in this large-format, full-color tribute to our ancient giants.

Nature Walks In & Around Seattle: All-Season Exploring in Parks, Forests, and Wetlands, Stephen R. Whitney
What to see along specific trails of parks and natural areas in greater Seattle. For all ages and walking abilities.

Nisqually Watershed: Glacier to Delta: A River's Legacy, David Gordon & Mark Lembersky
Seventy color photographs and text profile this model watershed and its influence on the area.

A Tidewater Place: Portrait of the Willapa Ecosystem,
Edward C. Wolf
Human and natural history of the Willapa Bay area of southwest Washington. Published by the Willapa Alliance with The Nature Conservancy and Ecotrust.

ABOUT THE MOUNTAINEERS

THE MOUNTAINEERS, founded in 1906, is a nonprofit outdoor activity and conservation club, whose mission is "to explore, study, preserve, and enjoy the natural beauty of the outdoors. . . ." Based in Seattle, Washington, the club is now the third-largest such organization in the United States, with 15,000 members and five branches throughout Washington State.

The Mountaineers sponsors both classes and year-round outdoor activities in the Pacific Northwest, which include hiking, mountain climbing, ski-touring, snowshoeing, bicycling, camping, kayaking and canoeing, nature study, sailing, and adventure travel. The club's conservation division supports environmental causes through educational activities, sponsoring legislation, and presenting informational programs. All club activities are led by skilled, experienced volunteers, who are dedicated to promoting safe and responsible enjoyment and preservation of the outdoors.

If you would like to participate in these organized outdoor activities or the club's programs, consider a membership in The Mountaineers. For information and an application, write or call The Mountaineers, Club Headquarters, 300 Third Avenue West, Seattle, WA 98119; (206) 284-6310.

The Mountaineers Books, an active, nonprofit publishing program of the club, produces guidebooks, instructional texts, historical works, natural history guides, and works on environmental conservation. All books produced by The Mountaineers are aimed at fulfilling the club's mission.

Send or call for our catalog of more than 300 outdoor titles:

The Mountaineers Books
1001 SW Klickitat Way, Suite 201
Seattle, WA 98134
1-800-553-4453